CUT THE CRAP ALREADY AND START CREATING THE LIFE YOU REALLY WANT

MANDY BARTON

Published by: Toprald Company, LLC

Printed in the United States of America

ISBN 978-0-9973608-0-6

MandyBarton.com

CONTENTS

PREFACE

The word *Purpose* gets thrown around a lot. Find your purpose. Live your purpose. What does it all mean? For me, purpose is the reason I was put on this earth. Purpose is simple. It is not always eloquent or impressive on the surface. I believe, simply, your purpose is something you can do forever and stay truly jazzed about. Purpose sounds different to each of us.

I was seeking my purpose for so long that, when I realized it was as simple as "Increasing the good of life around me," I almost discounted it. I used to think purpose had to be this big, complicated thing. That I'd have to travel to India and seek out a guru to find myself first. I didn't have time for that. So instead, I did all of the exercises, stayed in motion, and jumped countless times. And there it was.

Today, I can hardly believe my "luck" that I am going to increase the good of life around me for the rest of my life. And I see within it so many facets. In every area of life. I realized recently that I am living my dream life. Right now. The one I wrote about, prayed about, visualized, and created. By pursuing my purpose, I now spend time with people I want to be around, the ones I want my kids around, and, amazingly, I get paid for it. So will you. I'm talking super-high-quality time with friends who are creating big lives. These are people who are out there living this gift of life at level 10. I want more time with them, and, through living my purpose, I get it.

It's interesting how your dream life aligns with your purpose. You can live the life you work to create, just as I am.

And it's not in the future. It's right now. But I had to get started. I had to jump. And that's what this book will do for you. You don't have to know what to do or how to do it. There's no straight path, just action. Jump on it. Jump on the first thing you think of and then reroute, climb over, kick down, or go around. Whatever it takes.

My purpose is to increase the good of life around me. From the miniscule to the world-changing, when you take what is good and increase it, you, by default, leave less room for what is not. I have long since accepted and embraced that one of my gifts is getting people unstuck and roaring in the direction of their best self. By doing so, they increase what is good and begin to suffocate what is not. By doing so, they enable me to live my purpose and they go forth in theirs.

Wherever you're stuck, the answers are in here. The red flag to look for, to know when you are stuck, is the whole range from mild boredom or lack of motivation to pain and suffering, and everything in between. In other words, if you are *anything* besides on fire and excited about your life, you are stuck. Any sort of pain and suffering is certainly a sign you are stuck. But so is just being uninspired or simply not knowing what to do. You might need to be giving more. You might need to be receiving more. You might need to get loud. Whatever it is, I promise it's in here. Get ready to jump. Because that's what it takes.

And thank you for the part you play in increasing the good of life by picking up this book.

ACKNOWLEDGEMENTS

This book is dedicated to you who pushed and prodded me to take on an active coaching practice. Those who asked for thirty minutes to pick my brain. Those who signed up for anything I offered. Thank you. I would never have chosen to write a book without your eagerness and your willingness to demand more from life.

I acknowledge my parents, Ray and Linda Barton, for hitching their wagon to whatever crazy star I was chasing at the time. My mentor and dear friend, Gary Walton. My "work-spouses" and dear friends, Criss Wilson and Don McGehee. Lou Samara, my cherished friend and mentor. My first "big, scary hire," Vic Nance. Kim Keeling and the entire team at Barton Logistics.

For the work that they do or did, and the life-altering behaviors in me that they influenced: Gap International. The Rich Dad Company. Mary Kay Ash. Napoleon Hill. Jordan Adler. Harvey Mackay.

AUTHOR'S NOTE

Making the Most of This Book

This book sometimes makes references to God, the Universe, and Natural Law. It is not, however, a religious book. Pick the term you are personally the most comfortable with and don't get hung up.

This is not a "read it and put it away" kind of book. It's designed to be a manual and a blueprint. It's a book you read, and then do. Then read again, and do again. The chapters are designed to stand alone, as well as work together. Results take work, which is why at the end of every chapter, you'll find Jump Steps to take. Do them and you will get much more out of these lessons than you will by just reading.

Listen to the audiobook, in addition to reading, and you will reinforce what you are learning. This goes for any book, not just this one. The more senses you activate, the more you learn.

Organization toward any life of results is the key, so please create the lists I ask you to create, reflect when I ask you to reflect, develop the dream goals and write them all down. You can use your own notebook or use the *Step One: Jump Notebook* I refer to throughout this book. It's a system specifically designed for this program. You can order it online at www.mandybarton.com. More information is at the back of this book. Regardless of which you choose, your active involvement with this book is you being actively involved in creating your life. I want you to go for it. This is going to be fun.

CHAPTER 1

KEEP IT ON THE FRONT BURNER

I go to crazy lengths to keep the things that I know are important to my future on the front burner. What do I mean by that? Well, like cooking on a stove, the stuff you want to let simmer you put on the back burner. The food you want to cook at high heat, the stuff you need to pay attention to, you put it on the front burner. That pretty much accurately describes how I operate my life.

Many years ago when I read the book *Rich Dad, Poor Dad* by Robert Kiyosaki, it completely transformed my life. I had already started Barton Logistics and I was working tirelessly booking loads, finding carriers, and making sure that the freight in my care made it from point A to point B on time. That was our job. That was my job.

At least, I thought that was my job. After reading

Rich Dad, Poor Dad, I realized, actually those tasks were not my job. They were my employees' job. I realized that even though I owned the business, I was really acting like an employee in my own company. Wasn't I supposed to be out in front, leading it? Who was going to lead if I didn't? This was an awakening for me, but easily forgotten in the throes of a hectic day. Shippers would call, freight needed to move, and I'd look around. Everyone else was busy, so I'd handle it. An hour or so later, I'd remember, "Yeah, I'm not supposed to be doing that. I'm supposed to be providing all of the resources to make sure that gets done. I am supposed to be leading."

That was the moment when I decided a truth as important as "Don't be an employee in your own company" should never be on the back burner, not even for a moment. It should always be on the front burner, so that in the heat of the moment, when I needed that lesson the most, there it would be, front and center.

Before I tell you my trick for keeping things on the front burner, and top of mind, allow me to say, if you are not planning on keeping the things you learn from this book on the front burner, then you may as well close it now and do something else. Because we retain only about 10 percent of what we learn by reading, if you don't make this commitment, you will not likely be able to ever apply what you have read. You'll find it very difficult to improve your life and achieve your dreams. Dreaming is still very much alive, especially among very

Discovering what inspires you and keeping it on the front burner are the first steps to jumping.

successful people. But many of us don't remember how to dream, we're afraid to dream, or we were never taught. Some just dream with no commitment (this is also known as hallucinating, by the way) and it can be a very frustrating way to live or, at best, unfulfilling. This book will change that. Discovering what inspires you and keeping it on the front burner are the first steps to jumping.

When it came to *Rich Dad, Poor Dad*, that book was so important to me that I read it and reread it every month for a year. Every month! Then I reread it once a year for six or seven years. I've recommended this book to countless people, and, after they read it they remark and praise its transforming power. Then they go about their normal existence and do nothing with it. The problem was, they didn't reread it. We have to repeat our lessons to learn them. And that is my first trick for keeping those things that are important to you on the front burner: revisit and repeat the lessons until they are a part of who you are.

In practice, I'm no smarter than anyone else, but my life is a life of results. I put my mind to something and work it until I get the results I want. That's why people listen to me, why they come to me for advice and coaching. It's why they want to know how I did it. While other people are going on vacations, I take trips and attend seminars. Those rooms are often full of people doing the exact same thing. The difference between many of those others sitting in the chairs and me is that I keep

I put my mind to something and work it until I get the results I want.

the material that is important to me from classes I've taken and the books I've read in my face, on the front burner. It took some real creativity to do that. Life is cluttered. I'm human. I'm lazy, I avoid, I procrastinate, I'm fearful just like everyone else. So that leads me to the next trick for keeping those things that are important on the front burner.

The second trick is just that: know your tricks. What's your process when you know you have to do the hard thing? Do you jump right in? Or do you procrastinate, avoid it entirely, or make excuses? "Hmmm, before I jump into that, maybe I should just clean up my desk. Does the oil need to be changed in my car? Is the kitchen swept? Let me get a cup of coffee. I'll just answer this one email." Does this sound like you talking to you? What does your self-limiting trickster sound like? Pretty soon the morning is gone and you have effectively avoided doing the hard thing. This is me. This is most of us.

My way of solving this inevitable problem leads me to the third trick, which is creating ways to circumvent my well-honed skill of avoidance. Let me put it this way, it's very easy for me to put off the work I need to do toward a goal when that goal isn't top of mind. Sometimes I fall into this pattern not because I decided to avoid the task, but rather because I'm just doing other more immediate, usually less important, things that happen to be in front of me. They are on the front burner.

What's your process when you know you have to do the hard thing?

Most of my workday I spend sitting at a desk. One day, the idea hit me! I realized how I can keep important things in my face at all times. I went to the store and bought a digital picture frame. Most people put pictures of their vacations, friends, and family in those frames. They are good for that, too. But what they are really good for is keeping important goals, important messages, important concepts front and center.

My picture frame contains, for example, the saying, "The only thing missing is what I have yet to give." I learned that in one of the seminars I attended, and, for as meaningful as it can be to me, I would not have remembered it, it would not be a guiding light in my life if it weren't for the picture frame. And now that saying will not leave the picture frame until it is part of the fiber of my being. It has to be permanent, and I mean permanent, before it leaves the frame.

I wanted a second child and, until I achieved that goal, baby number two stayed in the frame. I'm just now learning that once I accomplish a goal, to leave that goal in the picture frame for a while to celebrate. That's hard for me, but more on that later. I'm getting better at celebrating and I push myself to not "delete" my accomplishments immediately, leaving them in the frame. I take the picture and stamp it "Accomplished," which reminds me to celebrate—again an important concept now on the front burner.

This picture frame trick is so simple and so powerful. What makes the frame different from a list or a static picture is, the images cycle and that motion catches your eye. It's easy to walk by a list, to push it to the side, to lay some other "important" paper on top of it. And regular pictures, the static ones sitting on your desk or credenza? Well, they easily become part of the office landscape. You barely see them after a while. But the digital frame moves, colors change, it goes from bright to dark, red to blue, and the eye can't help but notice the variations.

At Barton Logistics, we all have a picture frame at our desks. Now we all can put our most important things on the front burner. Let's face it, you're putting something there, so you might as well be deliberate about it. Choose wisely what you want to put in front of your face.

Get yourself a digital picture frame.

Make a list of tricks that your self-limiting trickster uses to derail you.

Load into the frame some tricks you can use to derail your trickster!

Then load a few actions you can take to shut that trickster down.

Later, you'll add a dream and some goals. But first things first.

CHAPTER 2

THE DREAM MUSCLE

We all have a dream muscle. We were born with it. I've found as you get older, though, if you don't tap into the dream muscle often enough, it atrophies. In the last chapter, I mentioned that many successful people are effective dreamers. I've become one of those, but I wasn't always that way. Long ago I completely shut off my ability to dream. When I graduated high school, my dream was to be able to pay my bills and be on my own. I followed through on it, got my degree from University of Texas, and accomplished that goal by age twenty-two. After that, I was lost. What was I supposed to think? "Okay, I can just die now?" I had nothing else worth striving to accomplish. I lost touch with that part of me that creates dreams. It's sad, but life does that to all of us sometimes. The "grind" takes over. I got so used to existing in a dreamless state of living—a "doing" state of living—that I was stuck, uninspired, and going nowhere.

It seems for many of us that losing the ability to dream happens in our twenties. When we are little kids, dreaming comes easy to us. A relative asks, "What do you want to be when you grow up?" And the answer might be, "I'm going to be the first woman on Mars!" That's a dream, unhindered by thoughts of how that ambitious child is going to get there; she is completely confident in her ability and certain it will happen. But by the time we get into our twenties, we often begin to have trouble. We lose our dreams and our drive. I've interviewed candidates for entry-level positions at Barton Logistics, young adults with their entire future ahead of them, who didn't have much in the way of dreams. Not completely horrible or unexpected, you might think. But it gets worse. The really sad part was when I would press the issue and ask these candidates to create a dream. They couldn't do it. They could not come up with one dream. You have to work the dream muscle just like you exercise any other part of the body to keep it in shape.

In all likelihood, some people are unable to dream because no one ever taught us what to do after we've accomplished a dream. The biggest enemy of success can often be success itself. Accomplishment, your dream realized, could have been getting your degree, getting married, having children, landing a good job, summiting a mountain, or achieving

You have to work the dream muscle just like you exercise any other part of the body to keep it in shape.

a certain level of income. All are real successes. But what next? No one puts any emphasis on the next dream, or to continuing to dream. Instead, you get caught up in the monotony of living. I sure did. That's when your dream muscle, my dream muscle, got weak. It is clear that many people, as they get older, stop dreaming. Part of the reason is, they get caught up in life. At other times, it's the fear of failing or not knowing how to achieve large goals. Both those reasons can feel overwhelming. Does that sound like you?

Here is a sure path to getting your dream muscle back in shape. And there's no avoiding this if you want to go anywhere in life. I've used this technique with people whom I coach at our company and elsewhere. The first step is to start with a small dream. Whatever that is. Then let your dreams get bigger after each dream you accomplish. Small dreams can be as simple as something you'd love to have for dinner—like king crab legs or a nice steak at a top restaurant. It might be something you'd really love to do next Saturday, like go horseback riding or finally clean out the garage. It could be something around your house that would be really cool if it were fixed. It might be that broken gate latch that drives you crazy every time you try to open it.

Each time you achieve one dream, your dream muscle gets stronger. Then you keep practicing this by allowing yourself to dream and then achieving until you start dreaming and achieving outside of your comfort zone. When you stretch, you get bigger

Once life starts getting better, there's no going back.

and your standards get bigger, too. That's how your life gets better and better. And once life starts getting better, there's no going back. Doesn't that sound like something you'd like to be in on? Doesn't that sound like something you can do? I know you can.

Dream and achieve. Dream and achieve. That's how the muscle gets stronger. And here's a little preview of a later chapter in this book: You don't have to know "the how" right away. Just get your dreams down and absolutely put them in the picture frame so you keep them on the front burner. You learned that in the last chapter.

One quote that has always really stuck out to me is this one by George Bernard Shaw: "The reasonable man adapts himself to the world. The unreasonable man persists in trying to adapt the world to himself. Therefore all progress depends on the unreasonable man." I'm asking all of you to be the unreasonable man and woman. Being reasonable gets you nowhere. Being unreasonable opens up your world!

You might be wondering how something like dreaming can play such a huge part in your success. Simple. It's the first step to making a better life for yourself and the people you love. People make this mistake all the time. They dream vaguely. They say things like, "I just want to be happy." Not good enough. Don't say, "I just want to be happy." Instead, ask yourself what "happy" actually looks like, what it may include and not include in your life. Be as detailed about your dreams as possible. Don't

Being reasonable gets you nowhere. Being unreasonable opens up your world!

be lazy about dreaming. Dreaming is a privilege, so take it.

If you're thinking your dreams will just happen on their own, ask yourself, "How is that working out for me so far?" People who are living the lives they want didn't just get lucky. Achieving didn't just happen for them. Anyone who is realizing happiness in their lives, who is making a difference in the world, or who is continually achieving success, started with a deliberate dream. Most likely they had many deliberate dreams. Read the history books. America as an independent country started with a dream. The cars we all drive started with a dream. There's nothing wrong with being a dreamer. In fact, there's everything right with being a dreamer. The dream muscle is a *yes* or a *no* box. Check one. Either you choose to dream, or not. Either you choose to accomplish what matters to you, or not. If you've convinced yourself that you don't have the time to figure out what your dreams are, or you don't have the time to live the life you want, well, that's your choice. But be careful. If you are unwilling to or can't put some teeth into your dreams, then you're checking the *no* box. And let's be totally honest: is dreaming or not dreaming really a matter of time? Perhaps your unwillingness or inability to dream stems from something more like fear, a feeling of unworthiness, or maybe a sense of being held back by someone in your life. Ask yourself, and then don't worry. This book addresses the crap we all wrestle with and shows you how to deal with it. You are not alone.

Dreaming is a privilege, so take it.

To all those people who can't or won't

take the leap to dream, who have checked the *no* box, I say, "Congratulations. You are setting yourself up for a life of mediocrity." And if that's good enough for you, well, that's your choice, at least for now. Eventually, when you really want something, you will shelve the excuses. But why wait? What exactly are you waiting for? So go ahead, with no delay, write down your dream specifically. You are allowed; you deserve this right. Take it.

List some dreams you accomplished in the past, ones that made you proud.

List some dreams you really want now.

List one dream idea that can serve as a focus for your next read-through of this book.

Put that dream on the front burner and in your picture frame.

CHAPTER 3

STEP ONE: JUMP!

Now that we have a few of the prerequisites out of the way . . . You have a dream that you'll keep on the front burner, and it's time to get busy. No dream happens without action. Even keeping that dream on the front burner won't get it done unless you act. In fact, not keeping a dream on the front burner and not acting is a recipe for frustration, sadness, even depression. So without further delay, it's time to jump into your future.

This chapter is the title of the book because, in truth, nothing can happen without step one, which is Jump! Making it to this page with a dream, and a commitment to keeping it on the front burner is the first step. You are in it; you just don't know what to do next.

Jump and build your wings on the way down.

I always say, "Jump, and build your wings on the way down." People who wait for their wings to be fully constructed, strapped on, and flight tested generally miss their opportunities to fly. And that's a shame, because if they had just jumped, they would shock themselves with their own ability to soar. In my experience, both my wings and my flight path always become real, but first I have to jump. Once I commit, the resources follow. Somehow in this world, it doesn't work the other way around. The resources never present themselves before you are truly committed. They never present themselves before you jump.

So you might be thinking, "That's a little scary." Of course it's scary, at first. Taking a leap of faith toward your dream can be scary—or it can be exciting, depending on how much you believe that resources follow commitment. And right now, you may not believe that at all. That's okay. Not knowing how you are going to achieve your dream and willingly declaring your intentions out loud takes courage. It takes faith. And it takes you truing up to your commitment, regardless of how it all plays out. You're going to be just fine.

Be warned. The two demons, fear and laziness, will get in your way. Overcoming them repeatedly, every time they show their faces is the only way you will be able to build your wings. Later, in the "Fear & Laziness" chapter, you'll learn how to conquer those demons. If you feel they are a big problem for you, and you are already seizing up, then skip to that chapter after you finish this one and read it right away. Then come

Both my wings and my flight path always become real, but first I have to jump.

back to this. You can read it again (and again) as a refresher when you come to it. Like I explained about my reading and re-reading of *Rich Dad, Poor Dad*, you may want to do that same thing here—that is, if you are serious about life and success. Lessons take repetition to sink in.

If there's something you want in life, how long are you going to wish for it? How long are you going to waste time? How long are you going to let fear dominate your life? It's time to draw a line in the sand and declare your goal to the world. That'll force you to put your butt on the line you just drew. Once you jump by declaring your intentions, you can no longer hide from yourself. Now you've got to make your word mean something.

Standing on the edge of a cliff not knowing whether you can muster up the courage to jump is torture. It's agony. The anticipation of all the things that could go wrong; the people who may disappoint you; the friends and family you'll have to face and announce your intentions to; the people in your life you fear may grow distant because you are growing, changing and taking on your own life. But here's the thing. The torture is in the anticipation; it's not in the doing. When you are caught up in the doing and in the action of accomplishing something, it's no longer scary. But when you are just standing there on the edge of "should I or shouldn't I?" thinking about the task at hand and all it could entail, that's when it's scary and overwhelming. Perpetually standing on the edge of

It's time to draw a line in the sand ... And put your butt on the line you just drew.

the cliff and looking down stops many people from living the life of their dreams. It stops them from living at all. Be comforted, though, my friend: action absorbs anxiety.

Understandably, jumping takes guts, but once you've done it, you've got something to work with. You've got some skin in the game. You can build your wings. And it is in that building that you build faith in yourself. My dad used to tell me, "If you work hard when you're young, you can have fun all your life." To me, he was saying, "Life is just going to get better and better the harder you work." There's never an end game. The real fun lies in building your wings while you are in action. What you accomplish ends up being icing on the cake; often, it's a lot more icing than you could ever see from the cliff's edge.

A moment ago, I said that once you jump, you have something to work with. If you're like many people, believing that truth may not come easily to you. A few things hold you back, and I speak from personal experience. First, not knowing your own mind and how it works against you absolutely holds you back. Yes, your own inner voice can keep you on the edge of the cliff indefinitely. It can even talk you out of your heart's desire. That's a recipe for regret.

Another hold back is not knowing how much you can actually achieve. I've found all too often we sell ourselves short and things aren't as hard as we make them seem. Finally, you hold yourself back by not having the bravery to push forward through your

Be comforted, though, my friend: action absorbs anxiety.

fear. Here's a revelation for you: You are the one who is limiting your life. You are the one limiting your achievement. It's not circumstances "out there." It's not the people whose opinions you fear. It's not anything beyond your control. You don't have to be able to see the whole path, dear one, you just have to get on it. Believe me, it will start to become clear. It has to when you're committed. Like driving on a road trip, you can't see the last exit you will take, just the next one and then the next one. Your job is simply to get on the road and keep moving.

If you don't believe me, wait until you achieve a real win. It's coming, and nothing else will have been different except how you perceived yourself to get that win. It was you, taking control. That's when you will realize it has been you all along—your mind building up barriers, holding you back from your dreams. Savor that moment, because it is extremely meaningful. And you'll gain tremendous power from it. Once you realize that you have the power to change your mindset, that you've had it all along and that it's the only thing really required, it makes winning that much easier. You gain all kinds of confidence.

The thing about growth is that you are the one who is always in your own way. Accept that truth. That's what makes growing hard, and at the same time that's what I love about it. Because it's me in my way, no one else. With that knowledge, I know I have the power to figure out how to get out of my own way, to do something about me.

The thing about growth is that you're always in your own way.

Changing me, changing my thinking, and saying, "Not this time!" to the self-limiting barriers my mind has conjured up is within my full control. And if changing me is in my full control, changing you is in your full control. It's true.

You might be saying, "Mandy, that might work for you, but there's no way this can work for me." I've been there, but I don't buy it. That would be like me saying that I can't learn something about investing from Warren Buffet or about real estate from Donald Trump because we have different upbringings and live very different lives. When you're engaged in the conversation of "That won't work for me because of this or that reason," then there is no room for the conversation that says, "*How can* this work for me, *how can* I have the life I want?" We are faced every day with the choice of which conversation to honor. The one that helps us grow, or the other one that keeps us small, and, in many cases, unhappy. Which is it going to be for you?

Here's another nugget for you. We get the answers to the questions we ask. So for the love of all things holy, STOP asking, "What else can go wrong?" STOP asking, "What now?" Do you really want the answers to those questions? START asking questions you actually want the answers to, such as, "How can I achieve this dream?" Put your most powerful asset, your mind, onto the task of a question worth answering. Trust me; your mind will figure out the answer.

I check my self-talk all the time, and I catch myself. Not long ago, I wanted to call a business leader because he had built a $100-million company and I wanted advice on doing the same with one of my businesses. I put that phone call on the back burner for five months because I was honoring the wrong conversation; I didn't know what I would say or how I was going to say it. I didn't know how he was going to respond. I was afraid to jump. Then I decided that I needed to honor the right conversation of, "How can I have the life I want?" rather than the wrong conversation of, "He won't want to talk to me because he's more powerful than I am." I called him in between errands. It wasn't a big deal at all; he was flattered, and he's now advising me with my business.

When talking to yourself, choose your words and conversation wisely. Then ask yourself this question: "If your golf caddy talked to you the way you talk to yourself, would you hire him or fire him?" Not a golfer? Then substitute hair stylist, doctor, or anyone you choose. Fire that caddy if you don't like the talk. You are the one in control, and most likely you are the one in the way of you achieving your dream. Your dreams are waiting. Jump already!

Your dreams are waiting. Jump already!

Write down what your inner voice is telling you and the questions it is asking you.

Then make a list of questions you really want the answers to and start asking them instead.

CHAPTER 4

NEVER, EVER, QUIT

I don't know what to say to people who quit—except, perhaps, "Stop doing it."

Who came up with the saying, "If at first you don't succeed, try, try again" and who decided that was good advice? Some of you may believe this saying encourages perseverance, but when you break it down, it really doesn't. "Try" implies you're not going to succeed! It only implies that you're going to try. Who has time for that?

My philosophy of never, ever, quit has been my secret weapon. And I believe it is one of the biggest reasons why I have been able to choose a dream, set out to achieve it, and actually get there. Not just once but many times in my personal and

The risk of true failure doesn't exist, unless you quit.

business lives. It is the weapon that no one knows I have. So when the naysayers underestimate me as I work to attain my next big goal, when they think I'm not going to get there, what they don't know is that I'm not going to quit. So I *will* get there.

People call these little sayings I have, like "Never, Ever, Quit," Mandyisms, and the power of this one is as simple as this: when you never quit, you can never truly fail. Too many people don't go after things they really want because they are afraid of failing. Well, what if you could pursue your dream and know that you couldn't fail? Would you go for it? You're still reading this book, so I know you most likely would.

So here's the big secret: the risk of true failure doesn't exist, unless you quit! When you take a shot that doesn't achieve the goal, you just learn another way that doesn't work. That knowledge moves you infinitely ahead. Let's say you want a house in a better school district for your kids. Your son is age one and your daughter, age three. Your dream is to make the move before they are ready to start elementary school. Would you drive that stake in the ground, jump, and announce that dream publicly if you were assured of achieving it? Of course you would.

For me, never, ever, quit is a state of being, a knowingness. It's a decision I make moment by moment, because it's in those weak moments—and we all have them—when never, ever, quit counts the most. It's peace of mind, a way of being, that when embedded in who you are, no one can ever

For me, never, ever, quit is a state of being, a knowingness.

take away from you. You simply know in your bones you are going to keep pushing forward. Never, ever, quit is your safety net. Make it your secret weapon. I know it's mine.

Figure out what you want, write it down, keep it on the front burner, and jump. I realize that's one of those "Easy for you to say, Mandy," kind of things. But at some point, you have to engage fully in the belief, "I can be great," stop talking about what you want, and get busy getting it. Otherwise, life is pretty miserable. And no one should choose mediocrity when they can choose happiness. You're going to work at your life one way or the other. Why not work at happiness?

I'm fully aware that there are people who haven't yet developed that "never quit" strength, and if you are one of them, this is my advice to you: make a plan. Make a solid plan for your future self when you begin to feel yourself getting weak. Decide how you are going to get yourself back on track to achieving your goal on that down-in-the-dumps day that's coming in the future. Put those words of wisdom to your future faltering self into your picture frame. Decide what else you are going to do to make yourself accountable. Don't let fear, laziness, or anything else defeat you. Listen to your self-talk and when that voice says, "It won't work for me, not sure I can do this," reply back, "Not hearing you today!"

When that voice says, "It won't work for me, not sure I can do this," reply back, "Not hearing you today!"

Sometimes you'll come across a part of your plan that is no longer working, or is ultimately not leading you to your desired end result. When you notice this, don't worry. Just tweak your plan a bit by tossing out what isn't working. Never abandon your real purpose; keep going with that. When you finally realize in your heart of hearts that there's no way you can abandon your dream, that it's just the plan that needs altering at times; that's when you know you've found your real purpose. It's an energizing, all-consuming, and wonderful feeling.

For some of you, confidence is an issue. Perhaps a loss you once perceived as a failure and not as a learning experience has stripped you of the confidence you originally had. Or maybe you didn't have an abundance of confidence to begin with. Well, here's the good news: achievement breeds confidence, and small achievements are the best way to get started. If your fear of failing is making you afraid to jump and achieve your dream—even a small one—confidence will never be yours. It's a vicious circle, and I see people trapped in it all the time. So here's how you break free: You start. You fake it. You announce, long before you believe it, "I am confident!" and say and act it repeatedly in your daily life until it's true.

My theory on confidence is, first you have to manufacture it for the sake of the life you want. It's a "fake it till you make it" game with yourself. You've got to constantly do the things that a confident person would do—like drive forward even though you are uncertain. Eventually, jumping will become a habit. Before you know it, you start to realize you are a confident person.

Achievement breeds confidence.

Before I close, I want to highlight a

pitfall you will likely encounter, and that's excuses. Some of you are still very impressed with just how spectacular your excuses are. Yay you! Making excuses doesn't feel like quitting, but in truth even when it's a "good one," you are quitting in that moment. Included in this book is a whole chapter on this subject. If you are prone to making excuses, then you may want to read that chapter next. For right now, however, recognize when you are allowing yourself to plan for excuses. Instead, put in your plan that excuses are unacceptable. It's an undeniable fact that you will lose every time you make an excuse, so let yourself off the hook if you want because, if that's the kind of person you want to be, then you are the one stuck living with that. Ouch!

Find yourself an accountability partner or group to help you when you feel like quitting. Or join the community over at www.mandybarton.com.

Put "I never, ever, quit." in your picture frame to keep it on the front burner.

CHAPTER 5

CREATE THE LIFE YOU WANT

I think the whole idea of a better life begins with knowing what you want. Or at least knowing that you don't want the rest of your life to be exactly as it is now. It's knowing, or, should I say, feeling your dream deep down in your gut. As you'll remember from the chapter on the dream muscle, dreaming isn't always easy for people. Dreaming requires us to place ourselves somewhere other than our present situation. For some, the thought is scary; for others, it's, "Why bother?" For others still, they don't know how to dream or have forgotten how to dream.

> **... put the time into figuring out what you want in life ...**

As you read this book, I'm going to ask you to put the time into figuring out what you want in life. It can be small or big. It might be both. Too many people miss this important part of the process. I'm going to ask you to put in the effort to picture the life you want and then begin. Right now. I'll guide you along the way. There may be some tough love, so be prepared.

Let's start with the life you want. You might wonder, or even hear others say, "I'm fine. My life is fine. I have enough. Why would I want anything more?" Or how about the uber icky, "I'm content. Why isn't that enough?" To that question, I'll answer simply: if you are not growing, you are dying. You are creating your life every day, and with every decision you make you are moving toward living or you are moving toward dying. Is this life that you are leading your ultimate ideal? If it is everything you ever wanted, and I mean everything, then great! But, when you look at your life—and be really honest with yourself—is there anything you would change? Is there anything you want that you don't have? Maybe a better job? A new car? Assets so you don't have to worry about retirement? Perhaps you'd like to be twenty pounds lighter, or twenty pounds heavier. Make a bigger difference for others, run a marathon. Would you like to have more time with your children, spouse, parents, or friends?

You can either put in the effort to live a life of abundance, or you can use the same amount of effort to live a life of deficit.

You get the idea. There's likely something that, if you really sat down and thought about it, you would change, or even aspire to. And since you are creating your life anyway, consciously or not, why not take the time to really design it? This is the difference between you leading life and your life of default leading you. I choose the first one every time. Either you're in control or you can abdicate it. It's your choice.

In my experience helping people who want to live a better life, I have noticed a pattern. A simple one, really, once you see it. And once you do see it, you might be like the folks I help, and choose controlling your life over letting it control you. The simple truth is, you can either put in the effort to live a life of abundance, or you can use the same amount of effort to live a life of deficit. In either case, you're spending the same amount of time and energy working toward whichever end you choose.

When you're living a life of abundance, for example, you spend your time having paid your bills, free to create what's next. When you live a life of deficit, you spend your time on the phone with the electric company asking for some grace, or you call to see which credit card company can give you a better rate on that large balance you're carrying, because you're a little short of funds and can't pay. You get the picture. What would you rather spend your time doing? Confidently paying your bills, or begging for a reprieve? You can spend your time making your dream happen or expend the same amount of energy buying into why it's hopeless. You're going to spend the time, so which is it going to be?

Many people make the choice, but it's the "doing" where a lot of them fall down.

Here's another one. Would you rather be clipping coupons and negatively living in the deficit-thinking mode or making money?

Some people will drive all over town to save three cents on a can of beans, all while wasting precious time, gas, and money because they believe they are saving money. You'll never create abundance by clipping coupons, folks.

The first choice is a life of deficit, the second a life of abundance. And make no mistake, they are choices you make every moment. They have nothing to do with who you are but they certainly can shape who you become. It is so much more important to grow your income and your world to match your dreams than it is to shrink your dreams to match your current income and your current world. If these choices reflect who you are, it's never too late to change. But you have to make the choice, and then do it. Many people make the choice, but it's the "doing" where a lot of them fall down. This book will help. It can keep you standing. It can keep you moving forward.

I'm assuming if you are reading this book, you want the tools to up your game. You want to have a life by your own design and are tired of a current world that seems to have "happened" to you. Understand this: you created your world and must accept responsibility. Also, understand that the great news is, you can change it.

If you want to change your current world, then keep reading. If you are still kidding yourself that you are perfectly fine the way you are, then go watch reality TV. That will certainly make your current life look better than the crazy lives of the people on those shows. But believe me, there isn't a successful person on this planet who isn't striving to do more and to do better, even now. That's how they became successful in the first place. You can be that person. I know you can because if I can, anyone can. But it's your choice whether you take the first step and turn the page—or not.

I'll leave you with this quote from one of history's most famous figures:

"It had long since come to my attention that people of accomplishment rarely sat back and let things happen to them. They went out and happened to things." —Leonardo Da Vinci

And this one sits in my digital photo frame: "Dear Life and Things: Let's get something straight. You don't happen to me. I happen to you. Love, Mandy."

**Think about that quote.
What does it mean to you?**

Picture what you want your life to be in five years and write it down (use the *Step One: Jump Notebook*).

Be specific. Picture everything, like how much money you have, what your day looks like, how much you weigh, who you are with, what you are doing, etc.

CHAPTER 6

THE OPPOSITE OF SUCCESS

It took me years to figure out that the opposite of success is not failure. It's mediocrity. The name of the game is eradicating mediocrity; it's not avoiding failure, folks. Failure is just a part of success. You are still in the game. You are not failing when you're screwing things up and learning from them; you're just still on the path to succeeding. So with this mindset your bar is set much higher. You can't just quit when you consider mediocrity the opposite of success. But you sure can quit when you think of failure as the opposite of success. In fact, that's why most people feel they failed—they quit. The truth is, quitting often gets you stuck in a life of mediocrity, rather than plummeting you into a life of

The truth is, quitting often gets you stuck in a life of mediocrity, rather than plummeting you into a life of failure.

failure. Think about that. Don't just skim over it. It is truly profound.

I've become so practiced in being blind to the notion of failure, and instead seeing the opposite of success as mediocrity, that when I see people living a life of mediocrity, of settling, of giving up, it makes me ill. To me it's a sin to not use your talents. It's a sin to not go for your dreams. It's like the Bible story about the servant who greedily buries his talents so they are of no use to anyone. I see it as a sinful, depressing, autopilot of a life. You've been called to more than that, and you damn well know it. Are you going to let fear-based mediocrity keep its hold on your life?

What do you say to the person who is living in the realm of mediocrity? They can be "successful" people, or they can be people hoping that either success finds them or they find it. Either way, they are people who are settling, asking, "What choice do I have?" Feeling as if their hands are tied. I see them as hostages to their current circumstances. And of course the reason is fear. Fear is the great limiter of people's happiness and dreams.

The first questions I ask people who are living a life of mediocrity are, "Are you really working this hard for average? For normal? And where do you think it will lead?" At best, I can tell you, it will lead to more mediocrity. I say mediocrity is a horrific disease, and the nicest thing you can do for this world is your part in eradicating it.

Mediocrity is a horrific disease, and the nicest thing you can do for this world is your part in eradicating it.

When we hear people and ourselves say that the opposite of success is failure, we are hearing words many people have come to believe are common wisdom. I call it what it is: a lie that gives you permission to run and hide. Failure doesn't feel very good, and it can be so devastating that many people never recover from it. It's an out to say, "I tried, and it didn't work out." That kind of statement gives us a nice, handy out, even if it is one we're not proud of. "Well, so much for that. I tried. I failed." And in the back of your mind, you know you're off the hook, perhaps miserably so, but off the hook.

For people in my company at Barton Logistics, if they are content being content, I say, "Great for you. But do it somewhere else. Mediocrity doesn't happen around me." I know that sounds tough, but let me show you how this plays out. I teach a class at the local library on finance and how to become financially free. It's the stuff I learned from many books and mentors, and have put into action in my own life. I also coach clients on how I did it, and these classes fill up within minutes of being offered. One of my clients needed coaching on his personal finances. It became very clear that he was on board and ready to move beyond mediocrity; his wife, on the other hand, was not.

He finally confessed that he wasn't implementing what he was learning because of the push-back he was getting from his wife. I reminded him, "On the first day of class, you didn't say you would accomplish your goal if your wife was on board. You said you'd accomplish your goal. That means the first time, or the 150th time, if that's what it takes. That means the first enrollment conversation, or ninetieth, if that's what it takes. You said you'd do it. So why are you waiting for anyone or anything?" He realized his wife was limiting his dreams and charged forward. After some time, and with a little more understanding and evidence, his wife is now on board. The truth is, if someone is on autopilot and you're on a mission, guess who wins? You do. But you have to be brave enough to confront your demons—remember "fear" and "laziness" from an earlier chapter. We'll go into more detail on that later, but for now recognize that when you are trapped in mediocrity where people hold you back, you have three choices: You can bring them along. You can zoom past them. Or, and this is the caution flag, you can succumb, you can settle and live a life of mediocrity. Are you going to lead your life or let other people who accept mediocrity lead it for you? If you choose the latter, stop reading this book and turn the TV back on.

When your dream is not just a dream, but a *commitment*, that's a game changer, my friend.

Another thing I realized about mediocrity as the opposite of success is that it keeps you in the process. You will experience resistance on the way to achieving your dream. Resistance is not failure. We'll talk a lot more about resistance in an upcoming chapter, but what you need to know

Are you going to lead your life or let other people who accept mediocrity lead it for you? If you're the latter, stop reading this book and turn the TV back on.

now is that resistance is just part of the process and it can knock you off course. Getting off course isn't failure, either. It, too, is just part of the process. So as soon as you realize you're off course, just admit it and course correct. No trauma, no drama, baby. Just get back on track. Case closed.

Once you are back on track and working toward your goal, you are back in charge of your life. And that's where you want to be. Any time you spend analyzing how you got off course, talking about it, questioning it, defending it, regretting it, denying it—all the B.S. we do—is just stalling. And stalling means you are off purpose. Make no mistake, stalling is moving backward. It's like the same Bible story where two servants used their talents and the third buried them. You're burying your talents in the ground through justification and idle talk. So don't spend time on why you got off track, just get back on track!

Thinking of mediocrity, rather than failure, as the opposite of success also helps limit your fear. How many of you are afraid of failure, of things not going your way? How often does that hold you back from change? When you plan for and welcome resistance and recognize that it will come with any choice you make to move forward, you are free to move beyond failure. You no longer have to feel bad about this natural part of the success equation. "Failure" is just more mediocre, status quo thinking and behavior that you will work past on your way to success. Fear not!

Now that you are starting to understand how I view success, mediocrity, and failure, and you're seeing how necessary it is to boldly free yourself from the status quo and those who will hold you back, you are arriving at the conclusion that this mindset is absolutely required if you want to live your dreams.

Allow me to caution you. You're a believer now. You see the light. You may want to move forward—badly! But the fear is still there and you hear yourself saying, "Maybe someday . . ." Or, "One day, I'll . . ." Or, "Once I get myself . . ." Or, "I'll take this on next year . . ." Stop right now. That is not success thinking and behavior. That is mediocre thinking and behavior in disguise. It is making excuses, and that is quitting in the moment. You remember that truth, right?

I will guarantee that everyone reading this book can think of some aspect of life where they are settling for mediocrity. Like I said, they very well may be highly successful in other ways. Sometimes that's worse, because when you have more to lose, the fear of breaking free from the status quo can be even more debilitating.

In my own life, I'm working to break free from my attitude and behavior of "I'll start looking for a life-long relationship and partner next month, or next year, or as soon as I'm ..." Once I move beyond this thinking, I'll move beyond a mediocre aspect of my life. I have achieved so much in my life, but not this—yet. Everybody has something.

Once you make the choice to move beyond mediocrity, your world opens up, and you live a life of your deliberate creation.

So let's stop striving for normal. Let's stop being afraid to move beyond average. When you declare to those people who are living in the realm of mediocrity that you are taking a stand and driving a stake in the ground, if they won't join you, you need to move on. That's when good things start coming your way. That's when the "how" that I often say, "To hell with," starts to present itself. More about that later. That's when you get inspiration and motivation and action beyond your supposed capabilities. Once you make the choice to move beyond mediocrity, your world opens up, and you live a life of your deliberate creation.

Make a list of everywhere you are settling for mediocrity in your life and keep it in your *Step One: Jump Notebook* as a reminder of the areas you will tackle.

Write down the steps you can take to move toward success in those areas. They likely will factor into your goals to achieve your dream.

CHAPTER 7

SO YOU DON'T HAVE TIME

So you don't have the time to create the life you want? Is that what you are saying when the words, "I don't have time," escape from your mouth? I don't have time to take that class. I don't have time to learn how to manage my money. I don't have time to exercise every day. I don't have time to really think about what I want in life, what my dreams are. No time to put some teeth into those dreams?

Are you kidding me?

Oh, and I should say, "Congrats!" You are setting yourself up for a life of regret. Apparently you have time for that. Sorry to be so bold so early in this book. Well not really. I know I sound harsh. The phrase, I don't have time, or its shorter cousin, I'm so busy, are just excuses, and not very good ones. You are quitting in the moment. Please listen to how often you say, "I don't have time. I'm so busy." Right now take out a piece of paper or use your cellphone or notebook. Track how many times you say it this week. Then reread this chapter to make sure you understand just how damaging "I don't have time" is. Recognize when you say it and then put it in the context of your priorities. Only you can decide what you're going to make a priority, and only you are going to make things happen for yourself.

"How?" you may ask, "With all I have going on?" Don't ask *me* how—ASK YOU HOW! Remember, in life you get the answers to the questions you ask. How about asking a question that will actually serve you? "How can I have time for this?" Let your brain go to work for you. That's really it. All you have to do is stop shutting your brain down by saying, "I don't have time."

I'm human. I do get it. I actually wrestle with this mindset, too, from time to time. Life gets busy, but what I've found is that if I really want to do something and if this *something* is really going to benefit me, then I find the time. But that's me. I've learned to take out all the massive time wasters in life, like TV, for example. You don't have time? Turn off the TV, deactivate your Facebook, and walk outside. If those activities are taking up all your free time and you can't find even an hour to work toward your dream, then it's time to cut them out. Take a break from all of the irrelevant stuff, the diversions that don't really matter, and you'll

The phrase, I don't have time, or its shorter cousin, I'm so busy, are just excuses, and not very good ones.

be shocked by how much time you recover in your life.

Remember, I get it. I have more excuses than most if I choose to take them. Not a day goes by that someone doesn't say, "I don't know how you do it all." I manage a working ranch. I run multiple growing companies. I'm a single mom raising two amazing kids. I homeschool. I have active investments. I'm a social being. I spend time with friends. I date. I'm accountable to my advisors. I coach others and travel a lot. I wrote this book; I read at least three new books a month; AND I still have time to eat, sleep, and exercise. All this, and I still manage to be out in front, actively *creating* my life. Did your mind just go to all the "Yeah, buts"? All the reasons I can do that, but you can't? Yeah, but you ... Yeah, but I ... blah, blah, blah. If I were spending my precious life minutes in the "Yeah, but" conversation instead of the "How can I?" conversation, I wouldn't have time either. Don't tell me you don't have time.

Stop saying "I don't have time." Just stop it.

CHAPTER 8

FIND YOUR LIMITING MOMENT

When I talk about finding the moment that limited your life, I'm talking about that one instance that shaped not only your life, but your belief about who you are. It may be a grand moment, but for many people the moment is tiny, completely insignificant to others around you at the time. In fact, those other people likely don't even know or remember that moment happened. But never mind, it shook you to the core, even if you didn't recognize it had that much power at the time it occurred. Unforgettable, perhaps it was a moment of shock, grief, reprimand, anger, or embarrassment, and it likely happened when you were a child. You probably have talked about it with others who are close to you, or maybe you pushed it deep down and tried to forget it happened. But if you take the time to search your heart, it will be there. Take some time to see if you know what I'm talking about, and if you don't already, this hint may help: the first thing that came to your mind was probably it.

The best way I can describe what I am talking about is to share a story about my own limiting moment. When I was in fifth grade, every Friday was pizza day in our elementary school cafeteria, and I loved pizza. One particular Friday, my friend offered me her pizza. So I ate her pizza and I ate my pizza. I really like pizza. No sooner had I downed the last bite than Miss Rickets, my fifth grade teacher, pulled me outside and said, "Mandy, that little girl doesn't get to eat at home. You have it really good at home. She doesn't. So I don't want you ever eating her pizza again." That was it. Meaningless to most everyone, except me. I built a life around that moment.

From that point forward I began to believe that I'm not going to go anywhere unless I can take everyone with me. For example, in the early days of our company when we moved into the little storage area at my parents' car wash, we really needed more surface area to work. I wanted to buy two bow-front desks. They're big desks with rounded fronts. But the space would not fit the two of them, which put me in a predicament. I didn't want to be the only one with a big desk, even though my employee said, "It's no big deal, you're the boss, buy the bigger desk."—I didn't buy that desk for a long time. I wasn't going to do something for myself without taking my employee along.

So what is your limiting moment? Mine was shrinking to protect others ...

I don't blame Miss Rickets for any of this, by the way. I'm the one who took from her reprimand the belief that I owed everybody and that I couldn't move up unless I helped everyone else move up, too. She didn't say that, she didn't say anything like that, but that's what I heard and what I made it mean—that I owed everyone for my good childhood and my good life. That belief defined who I was and limited me for a good thirty-five years. Even well after I started Barton Logistics. Now that I've identified this moment and I am past it, the amazing thing is, people are coming with me on my own journey upward. I don't have to drag them or convince them or shrink to wait for them; they willingly come with me.

I made the decision in my life to not stay small. I made it clear to myself that I had no intention of waiting until I could bring everyone with me. And guess what? The people around me are getting bigger. In fact, I've discovered that people are *huge* and there is no reason to play to their smallness. All that from a darn piece of pizza in fifth grade that I didn't even ask for! Because of that, I owed everyone for my good childhood and my good life—for the majority of my life.

That belief defined who I was and limited me for a good thirty-five years.

So what is your limiting moment? Mine was shrinking to protect others, if I had to put it into words that describe how I often felt. Once you discover your limiting moment, you'll be better equipped to see how it has played out in your own life. And once you see how your feelings have manifested into a pattern of behavior, you can decide whether your interpretation of that moment was legitimate, or not; whether it has served you well in life, or not. Whether it is going to serve the person you want to be, or not.

Now you have a choice. You can say, "That's not how I want to live my life. That's not how I want to be defined. That's not who I am." Choose a real truth based on another, more positive moment. One that empowers you rather than limits you. Or heck, just make one up. I mean, you made up what the limiting one meant, anyway. Make up something else about a positive one! It's not that hard. Why not choose a positive interpretation of a defining moment over the negative one? It's ridiculous to choose the negative moment, when you think of it that way, but we all do it.

If you are having trouble coming up with your current limiting moment, ask yourself what you want out of life and define it. Then examine your current beliefs, throw out the ones that don't support your dream, and keep the ones that do. Ask yourself what would be different in your life if you didn't cling to those thoughts that are holding you back. For me, I realized believing I had to take everyone with me was causing me to move slower than I wanted toward achieving my dreams. In fact, I was living a smaller good than I wanted at a much slower pace, rather than the bigger good that I knew I had in me. It was frustrating achieving at the pace of my slowest friend, family member, or business

Choose some other truth based on another, more positive moment, one that empowers you rather than limits you.

associate. And sadly, some of them were not moving at all; some of them didn't even want to come with me but they wouldn't tell me, "No," so I just kept trying to pull them along. So where did that leave me? You guessed it. On the shoulder of the road with the flashers on. Just waiting. And waiting. Think of those flashers as a wake-up call that the world—your world that could be—is passing you by.

Today, I absolutely demand that if you are going to stay in my space, you have to grow. And I am not going to wait for you. Others have to keep up with me! Suddenly, my desire to help people grow is more effective. Waiting for them wasn't nearly as powerful as charging ahead. All this has come through examination of my limiting moment.

So when you are ready to put this book down, I encourage you to write down your limiting moment and ask yourself, "Is your interpretation of it working for you? Is it is getting you where you want to go?" If you are happy where it has led you, great. If not, then it is time to make a decision and choose a new moment, or choose a new interpretation of that moment, one that will take you where you want to go. I believe this awareness and the choice that comes with it will transform you, as it did me. It will turn you into the person you want to become, help you achieve your dream and bring others you care about—and who truly care about you—right along with you.

What limiting moment or moments can you identify in your life? Write one or more down in your *Step One: Jump Notebook*.

What moments hold the potential to serve as your more empowering replacements? Write these down, too.

Read them and recognize that the moments on the first list are beliefs you conjured up from a real-life experience. The moments on the second list are also real-life experiences. Which ones hold more water? Precisely the point. You get to choose the ones that empower you.

Figure out how you are going to reinforce these new beliefs and interpretations. I loaded mine into my digital picture frame.

CHAPTER 9

FIND YOUR PURPOSE

If finding your limiting moment is important, imagine how powerful it can be to define that thing that you were put on this planet to do. It's amazing what a strong purpose can do for your drive. Particularly as you pursue your dream. All that self-talk we do, those words in our head that we use to undermine ourselves, they wouldn't be there as often if our purpose was strong enough and we were actively living it. People find it hard sometimes to find their purpose. They get all confused and mixed up. Is it about doing what I love? Is it about doing something that matters? Is it about money?

Where are you having an impact? Why are you doing it? The answers to those two questions hold the key to your purpose.

Finding your purpose doesn't have to be that complicated. Where are you having an impact? Why are you doing it? The answers to those two questions hold the key to your purpose.

The hard part is, we often don't *see* the impact we are making ourselves. As you evaluate your own efforts, you may find it really hard to take a step back and see your true impact. The impact muscle is one we need to exercise along with the dream muscle that we talked about earlier in this book. Too often we sell ourselves and the good we do short. If you haven't got a clue on the subject of your own impact, you can do two things: You can make a point of taking note when you felt like you made an impact. And you can ask some of the people around you. If you do the latter, be sure the people around you are the right people. If you are unsure about that, hang tight because the next chapter covers this very subject. The five people you spend your time with will be your future, not your past.

Once you find your purpose, it will energize you. So what is a purpose, exactly? For starters, it is something you can do forever. For example, I never tire of constantly improving on the good of life around me. That's my purpose and I can do it forever. It brings hope, meaning, and contribution to my world and the bigger world around me. It is now a healthy, positive manifestation of my limiting moment.

Your own purpose is a big thing. When it's right for you, you'll live it every day, and you'll do it everywhere. Once you've found your purpose, you won't ever feel like you've had enough time to work on it. It becomes like breathing, both necessary

So what is a purpose exactly? For starters, it is something you can do forever.

and natural. I'm going to choose to continue breathing. That's how much of a non-choice it is.

I always look a bit sadly on those people who never find their purpose. My father, my hero, never found what he loved. There was a time he really enjoyed the engineering and drilling side of the oil business, but that wasn't his purpose. He was a great supporter in helping other people light their own fuses and helping them find their own purposes, especially mine, but he never found something that really called to him. I suspect his calling was to enable the greatness in others, but I don't think he ever got hold of the right words for him. There is power in knowing the words that define what you were put on this earth to do. It's worth spending some time on. If you choose to not seek your purpose, then what will be your alternative? A life of mediocrity or living with your purpose?

You'll find your purpose in the most unexpected places. And you'll deliver your purpose in unexpected places. From the grandiose to the seemingly mundane. It's like the road trip mentioned in an earlier chapter, you see more and more of it the further you go.

Make a plan to discover your purpose. This can be one of the goals you write in your notebook.

To help you get started, ask yourself where you make or have made an impact.

Reflect on what jazzed you about making that impact.

Schedule it! Commit to getting your hands on the words of your purpose. Bring in a coach if you need assistance.

CHAPTER 10

THE FIVE PEOPLE

In the last chapter, I mentioned that the people around you can help you discover your purpose. The truth is, the people around you can help you with a lot of things. One of my favorite exercises to teach and to personally do is called "The Five People." Not only do I lead this exercise for the people I coach, but also for my own benefit. And I do it often, just to make sure I am on my path and not straying. People play a big role in that. Ready for the exercise? Take out your iPad or a piece of paper or a napkin or anything else so you can jot down one of the most enlightening lists you will ever create. Ready? I want you to write down the five people you spend the most time with. Don't count your young children; however, do count your older children. If there is one thing in

If there is one thing in this book that will really resonate with you, this is it.

this book that will really resonate with you, this is it. It will surely stick. I'll wait for you to create your list ...

I want you to take a look at that list and hear this truth loud and clear: This list represents your future. The future of your physical, moral, financial and emotional health. If you're okay with the future you see in front of you in the form of these five people, and you're truly happy with your list—meaning it represents the future that you want—then you may skip this chapter. However, if you're like most people, including myself several years ago, then your list is pretty alarming. And if your list is like mine was, it may even be scaring the heck out you right now. Take a breath.

The next step can be a bit tricky, but it is necessary. It's time to bring different people in your life, so get ready to start a second list. But who, you might be wondering. The best way to start is to think about people in your periphery whose lives you really admire and want for yourself. Don't think about cutting the people who are on your current list out of your life. This isn't about eliminating people. It's about trading your time. The people whose lives you admire get more time and the others may naturally get less. This doesn't have to be about who's right versus who's wrong, and it doesn't need to be a sit-down conversation with any of them. You are just making a conscious choice about bringing more of what you want into your life.

The goal here is to bring in the good, not get rid of the less good.

When I first did this exercise, I saw some people on my list, including some family members, who didn't portray my ideal future. They weren't wrong, it was just me deciding that in the context of the future I wanted, their lives were not necessarily lives that I aspired to. So I looked for ways to add time with people who inspired me and were living in a way I aspired to live. That conscious decision changed the course of my life.

Compiling my second list, I wracked my brain trying to figure out whose life I wanted and admired. Who do I want to get closer to in the context of my future? Who do I know whom I want my life to look more like? This was hard for me. It took me a while because the list of people worthy of my time is extremely important—it's critical. But I also didn't know very many people who fit the bill of what I wanted my future to look like, and that was a big problem. When I made the second list, some people on it were barely acquaintances. How was I going to get them into my circle? It turns out it actually was easier than I'd thought it would be. It's amazing how effective it was to simply reach out and ask these folks to lunch, volunteer for the same organizations, or join boards they were on. Entering their lives was much easier than I had imagined. This was me deliberately going for a life of my own creation.

In all the times I've led this exercise, not once has somebody been completely satisfied with their first list and the future it represented. I've had people looking at their list

In all the times I've led this exercise, not once has somebody been completely satisfied with their first list and the future it represented.

literally vocalizing out loud, "This list scares me if it's my future!" And that's fine, now that you're aware. I've come to discover nearly everyone can use an upgrade. Before creating their lists, everyone was fine and happy, but when we put that list of people into the context of "this is your future," then that's when things get real. They are characters in your current reality. Is this the reality you want for the future?

Nearly everyone also has difficulty coming up with the second list. It's not easy. I once spent three hours in a hotel room in Bay City, Texas, making my second list. It was a brain wrenching experience to list people whose lives I wanted mine to resemble. It came down to who it is that I envy. Many people think envy is a bad thing and I suppose in some applications it is. When it comes to envy, though, I'm honestly grateful for it, because envy points me in the right direction. I always say my jealousy points me straight and I'm honestly grateful for anyone with a life that makes me jealous! It tells me quite clearly what I want in life. But rather than let it consume me, I make a conscious choice to create that reality for myself.

It happened faster than you might think, but the people on that list I created that night are now in my life. Seventy-five percent of them are accessible, half of them I would call friends. That night, I made a deliberate upgrade for my kids and me. When I took a real look at my first five original people, regardless of what great people they were and are, I realized that in the context of my family's and my own future, this group of people were not what I wanted. My life and the way I spent my time needed an upgrade.

The goal here is to bring in the good, not to get rid of anyone. We're choosing to spend more time with those who have lives we admire and who we aspire to be more like. As life changes, I remake the list, and I'm constantly seeking to bring into my world more people I admire. I'm on the prowl for greatness in others. I'm shameless about it, I'm flattered when others want to bring me into their circle for that same reason. I don't apologize for being forthright about doing it for myself.

So you've made your second list. Now what? Now, you get in front of these people any way you can. It's time to get creative. As I mentioned earlier, join the same committees they are on, find some mutual ground, ask them questions, or grab a lunch. Make the nervous phone call and offer your help rather than ask for theirs. Making that call and putting yourself out there might be one of the hardest things you've ever done. Fear and laziness will hit you right between the eyes. But few things are more critical than this; it's your future. These people on your list are your future teachers. Figure it out. Some will likely be in your periphery anyway or how would you know their life inspired you? Whatever it takes, be bold. Just get strong and approach them. Many times, they are flattered.

I'm constantly seeking to bring into my world more people I admire.

If you are having trouble creating your second list, then you have a different problem. I've seen this before. Difficulty coming up with any names at all means you are not engaged enough in life and engaged with enough people. You may be a bit of a loner and that will not serve you well in terms of realizing your dreams. If this is you, then before you can create your second list, you need to start putting yourself out there. Start by volunteering or serving on a board. I always suggest volunteering because you're giving back. More on that in a chapter to come. Just know for now that you get what you give, and you can't out-give God. The more you give, the more opportunities and blessings come back your way. It's a natural law of the universe. If you are not a giver, then you are going to have a really hard time receiving any abundance from others. The others who are your future.

List the five people who get the most of your time right now, recognize that they are your future, and decide if you are okay with that.

Identify people you would like to have more time with and take action toward that end.

CHAPTER 11

TO HELL WITH NAYSAYERS. FOR THEIR BENEFIT

May I share with you how freeing it was the day I finally said, "To hell with the naysayers!" and meant it? And not only meant it, but realized it was my job to lead the way, despite their naysaying. I decided that rather than shrink to their reality, I would instead create an environment of opportunity for them and others. Sometimes, all people need is an eye toward the opportunity that is around them. Naysaying is really not much more than close-mindedness. It's people not believing something is possible or acceptable until they see it and it is accepted by others.

Let me share with you my story. I wanted to start a family, and my biological clock was ticking. I had no long-term man in my life, and dating, well, it wasn't delivering anyone of husband material. So I could have just given up on my dream of having children or waited and waited and waited until who knows when, if ever. But I didn't do either of those things. I decided to have my children through science, not fate. Deliberately. So today I have two amazing kids born of a sperm donor and me, through in vitro fertilization.

Let's face it, having my kids the way I did, in a small, close-knit town, is a recipe for chatter. And the chatter was rampant. "Mandy is pregnant? With who? She did *what*?" Of course, many people, maybe most, were just plain happy for me.

I love all of these people after all. Many of them I have known all my life. Eventually, I began to notice something about the naysayers. When I took these—in their minds—outrageous leaps in life, made these deliberate choices toward my dream, and was successful in business and in life, something interesting started happening. By me not limiting my growth and dreams, I began to realize I was helping others not limit their own growth and dreams. I saw my making these choices as an opportunity both for myself and for the people, including the naysayers, around me. I was unknowingly beginning to turn smallness—theirs and mine—into greatness first by jumping, then following my own path and believing in people, even if they

I decided that rather than shrink to their reality, I would instead create an environment of opportunity for them and others.

didn't yet believe in themselves. That idea appealed to me and it reached well beyond just family planning.

Naysayers can stop you from getting the life that you want. "What will people say?" you might fear. "What will they think of me? Will my family be supportive?" The fear of being called out is too much for those who do not yet realize that their own leap toward their dream is an outward invitation for others to make similar leaps in their lives. For every one naysayer there are ten people who think I am the bravest, most amazing person for the choices I have made.

Naysayers, and the gossip they generally cause, aren't limited to small towns. Living in a big city is no different. You still have your own personal small town, that same small circle around you. You frequent the same places, live out the same routines, and can be caught up in the same small, limiting reality. It doesn't matter where you live, you will have naysayers in your own circle. Families, friends, protectors of the status quo, people who wouldn't even consider themselves naysayers. They believe they are "protecting you from yourself." They are protecting you from foolhardy behavior, from wanting too much, from being hurt, from working too hard, from being unrealistic, from ... The list goes on and on. What they are actually doing is inhibiting you from achieving your dream while they protect their own reality and view of the world. Naysaying is a very self-protecting, self-limiting behavior. Your life staying the same—or small—keeps them

Naysayers can stop you from getting the life that you want. "What will people say?"

feeling secure in their own lives.

The personal value in not letting naysayers' words affect you is that you don't waste time with anger and hurt. You just keep going, keep growing, and you can take naysayers along with you. Here's a window into how I enact that belief in my life, and I see it become reality constantly. I am aiming for great wealth, and I'm building toward it every day. That's a decision I made, and I want to offer people a chance to come with me. That's why I teach classes at the local library, why I coach people, why I grab a coffee with someone who wants my advice. If I'm succeeding, they can succeed. I was not born with any more advantages than they; in fact, maybe fewer. Where I'm headed, I can't even see because it's so out in orbit. My advice to them is jump on board now before you perceive where I am as unreachable. There is a sense of urgency here. I want people to participate in growing. Then I want those people to bring others with them until we've all created the individual worlds we want.

One of the biggest personal discouragements I hear from the naysayers is, "Mandy, when is enough, enough? How much do you really need?" Or, "More money? Really?" None of those questions are relevant. I know I am a completely different person from the one I used to be, and I'm giving back to the world more than I ever could have otherwise because of how far I have come. With wealth you can create prosperity, schools, entrepreneurial classes,

When I hear and see the naysayers, all I really see are people who need help, who need someone to help them dream and believe in those dreams.

and, maybe one day, eradicate poverty. That's not a quick task, it can't be done by Monday, but I can certainly help eradicate the poor mindset. I can do that right now. So the real question for me is, "When is enough giving enough?" And the answer is easy: Never! Not until there are no more people in need. What I work to help the naysayers understand is that it's not about, "How much do I really need?" but "How much can I possibly give?" And the answer is, it's never enough. Regardless of what they say, I'm doing this. They can jump on board or happily naysay their lives away. I'm okay with their choices.

I discovered years ago that a big part of my dream is helping as many people as possible find their own dreams and live theirs. It all started with that pizza in the school cafeteria, you may recall. That starts with me. You want to help people? Help yourself first and show them how you did it. I want to build wealth, and that's going to require more of me than I have right now. I'm okay with that—actually excited by that—because I'll grow in the process. When I hear and see the naysayers, all I really see are people who need help, who need someone to help them dream and believe in those dreams. They need someone who can show them the path to growth by example. I'm that person. And I refuse to give up on them. I'll set the example and I'll take the backlash. I hope that, eventually, they'll see it's an abundant world. If they don't, whatever. Everyone can be rich and live a rich life, however you define it. We can be that

Naysayers are gifts to your forward progress.

example. We're creating wealth all the time, and if there isn't enough, then we will create more—despite the naysayers and for the naysayers. Naysayers are gifts to your forward progress. Will your loved ones be supportive of your crazy commitment to this journey? They will if you are loud. . . .

Resign yourself to prove the naysayers wrong.

Be humble about it, because the goal isn't to say, "I told you so," but to set the example so they can find their own dream and believe they can live it.

Assume the stance, "If I can do it, you can do it." And even though the work is hard, show them the path is simple.

CHAPTER 12

BE LOUD

You can get away with anything when you're loud. Loud means putting yourself out there and having no apologies for going for your dream. You do it knowing you're not perfect, admitting that you don't know the way, and recognizing that none of that matters. It's saying, "I know the direction of my dream, and I'm going very boldly in that direction." This is about talking the talk and walking the walk in a very loud way.

My small 2.5-children-and-a-dog-per-household community has completely embraced my unconventional choices, which include choosing to have my two children through science while I search for Mr. Right; owning Barton Logistics, a company in the traditionally male trucking world; and living on a

You can get away with anything when you are loud.

nice-sized ranch. They embrace me for one reason: because I'm loud. I'm transparent. I'm not hiding a single, solitary thing. I'm not embarrassed or guilty because of how much I have and how big, crazy, and "out there" my goals are. I don't hide how I came to start my family and how I raise my kids. It doesn't do them or me any favors to give in or stay small. That kind of behavior just isn't loving.

My life is not the norm by any standard. I live on a ranch and raise not cattle or sheep, but wild African hoof stock. Plenty of people asked, "How in the world are you going to take care of gemsbok, kudu, and wildebeests? Traditional livestock would be a lot easier." My answer was, "I don't know. I'll figure it out." And, of course, I have, because this was something I committed to doing.

Being loud knocks people back onto their butt, and gives you a path to walk through. Particularly the gossips and the naysayers; they get completely knocked down. Loudly living your life, unapologetic, driving for whatever it is you want renders the haters and the derailers powerless because your results refute all their criticism.

You can only imagine the amount of social criticism and personal hurt I could have experienced because of my personal life choices. Making the choice to be a single mom, loudly. Overtly showing the world that I was unwilling to deny myself the joy and the right to be a mother because I hadn't yet found the right man. I was a thirty-five-year-old woman who knew she wanted kids, so I went for it. Twice,

Being loud knocks people on their butt

actually. I have two amazing kids, whom I love with all of me and who absolutely would not be here if I hadn't decided to live life loud.

I've grown to live this loud life because it not only helps me create the life I want, it creates this sort of wake in front of and behind me, like I'm some sort of boat cutting through the water. Or maybe I'm channeling my inner Moses. That wake parts the seas of conventional thinking. And the louder I am, the bigger that aspect of my life is, which gives me and others a clearer path to live our dreams, whatever they may be. Why shrink because of what others might think? That's not truing up to yourself. When you're loud, you boldly give yourself permission, time, and space to do whatever it is you set out to do.

Because of my choice to be a single mom, it's my joy to liberate other women who are single moms by circumstance rather than by choice. By me loudly defying what some may call logic, abandoning traditional expectations, and insisting on becoming a mother my way, it has actually cut the cord called *stigma* for a lot of single mothers. They tell me they now feel they have the freedom to be proud about their circumstance if they choose. And doesn't a proud mother have a greater chance of being a better parent? Doesn't loudly loving your child and your life make for a better relationship and happier home? Of course, it does when you consider the alternative: embarrassment, shame, regret. Those

When you're loud, you boldly give yourself permission and time to do whatever it is you set out to do.

aren't feelings I'd want around any kid.

When I made the decision to go through in vitro fertilization, it was my leap, not the townpeople's leap, not my family's leap. It was all mine. The last thing I wanted was for others to take my unconventional choice out on my kids, whispering in their presence, remarking, or wondering. I couldn't hide in the shadows. That would have just opened the door for hurt. Instead, I got loud about my choice, demonstrating how it was part of my personal life design, which, of course, it is.

In the early days, people would imply that finding a man would be tough because of my two kids. My reply then was simple: "When my life partner shows up, he'll see my two kids and my third kid—Barton Logistics—as part of my appeal, along with whatever other crazy things I've conjured up by then." Living loud has quieted that question over the years. I've had others tell me that it's going to take a very big man to take on my two kids and me. Only small thinkers would equate two kids and a strong woman as something to "take on" as if we are some kind of baggage. Actually, my life choices and the way I live are great sorting mechanisms to weed out the wrong people. Living loud allows me to live my life choices fully with people who are living loud, too, and taking on life. It's where I want to be. And it's who I want to be with.

Insist on living life your own way, and doing the hard work to figure out what your way is.

The reason is simple. Now that I've chosen this route for myself and I've witnessed all the good that has come from my choices, I have found great joy and fulfillment. Insist on living life your own way, and doing the hard work to figure out what your way is. That's the dream many of us have forgotten about. When you finally make the choice and do things your way, loudly and with massive action, the world falls in line behind you.

Actions are important—I call it "getting big," and we'll go over that in the next chapter—but so is being loud about them. Being loud sets other people free and, through example, gives them the permission to decide their own dreams and live them.

What we are talking about here is choosing, and then boldly going for whatever dream you choose. It's taking a leap of faith not knowing how you are going to achieve it, but knowing for certain that you will. Understand, this takes real bravery. You're heading full force toward the unknown, and you've driven a stake in the ground about it. Loud means you are determined to make your choice gloriously work for you, no matter what happens. At first, you may need to bluff your way through it until you get a few victories. But then, with that positive reinforcement, be confident and loudly go after the achievement, the life you want.

What we are talking about here is choosing, and then boldly going for whatever dream you choose.

Keep in mind, the advantage you have is your "never, ever, quit" promise to yourself. That's a decision, too, and knowing that you're never going to give up also gives you more confidence. It's a true testament that the only end result is going to be success.

Of course, you will have people telling you otherwise. That's okay; expect it. Because when you get to where you're going, instead of saying, "I told you so," you're going to say, "Come along." Living loud is about creating that wake in front of and behind you. "Come along" invites others to ride your wave of happiness, prosperity, or whatever, and find their own dreams. You have an opportunity to impact more lives this way.

The naysayers are there to push you off course, and often they are people you love. You have to push right back, and in the end they will be better for it because they will witness you, the living embodiment of living your dream. And they will see it as good, and perhaps enviable. As I have said, envy isn't a bad thing; it helps show us what we want out of life.

Naysayers are not worthy of your anger, but they are worthy of your help through you living loud. They often respond only to visible proof, and you're it. The way I see it, naysayers have grown to be negative, small-minded, and limited people because they themselves have been limited. The most loving thing you can do for them is continue on your path, get loud and do what you're going to do regardless of what barriers lie in your way. Then invite the naysayers to come along when you've arrived. If they don't, they don't. Whatever.

Naysayers are not worthy of your anger, but they are worthy of your help through you living loud. They often respond only to visible proof, and you're it.

The nicest thing you can do for the people who truly love you is be deliriously happy. After all, what do you want for your precious loved ones?

When you become the kind of person who creates your own world the way you want it, it in turn inspires more people to do the same thing. You lead by example, and you give others permission to let their own light shine. If I had been small and had given into the laziness with my personal life or my company, if I had shrunk to pacify the naysayers, I would not have accomplished all I have so far. And I would not have two precious kids. Just as importantly, no one around me would believe they could accomplish much more than what they were currently living in their lives, either. Instead, I became a person who is capable of making these enormous changes. Others see that because I am loud. They begin to believe they can live the life they dream of, too. You can play the same inspirational role and achieve your dreams at the same time.

Everyone, including myself, has had friends and family members in the midst of something awful. You may know someone who is suffering right now. My way of living loud has allowed me to be a resource for them. They know I've been through a lot of challenges myself and have found ways to create opportunities. I often happily guide them toward a whole new world simply by choosing their dream and then living that choice loudly. They just needed a

I made the decision to be loud before I believed I had any right to be that way. So that's step one. Just decide ...

real chance, and now that they have it, they might just achieve more than I ever have.

So how do you live loud? I made the decision to be loud before I believed I had any right to be that way. So that's step one. Just decide, as I did, to become that headstrong person who sees things through. I painted myself into such a corner by being loud that I had no other choice but to produce. And a little pressure never hurts when it comes to achieving your dream. Every last person is capable of doing the work, and building confidence along the way. So drive that stake, declare your future, and true yourself up to it. Start behaving like you have already arrived, and be mindful of that little faltering voice asking, "Who do you think you are?" Self-awareness of your thinking is how you stop those inevitable negative thoughts. Be your own coach, call yourself out on thoughts that will undermine you, and be loud.

Write down what you will say when people ask about your dream, and memorize it. This is a step toward achieving that goal.

Practice it so that it rolls, not just off your lips, but is part of who you are.

Start and keep a list of the negative stuff people who are still settling for mediocrity will say, and how you'll respond.

Practice those answers, too, or better yet, practice not arguing or defending, and just charge ahead anyway.

CHAPTER 13

GET BIG

In the last chapter I said you have to be loud about your dreams and your life. I also stated you have a choice: you can either shrink or get big through the process. That was a preview of this chapter and a natural follow-up to being loud. Once you decide to be loud, you have to get big. Now the fun begins.

Nowhere did that play out more than in my business. In the early days of Barton Logistics, I was not a successful business owner. Barton Logistics was a tiny, one-person freight brokerage, operating in an industry of giant competitors. Even though I was struggling, no one would have known. Every day, I woke up and put on the face of the successful business owner. Then I lived it to the best of my ability, handling the resistance and the problems as they

Once you decide to be loud, you have to get big.

came my way. I acted big, and got big, before I was big.

In my personal life, having my children on my own through in vitro fertiliazation is unorthodox. As I noted earlier in this book, I decided not to wait for a husband, and instead listened to my biological clock. I wanted to make sure I achieved my dream of being a mother and didn't want that dream to be *only if* I had a husband. That's conditional language, and I don't buy into that. My dream was my dream. It wasn't contingent on certain conditions like being married. It was contingent only on me; it was based only on my willingness to drive a stake in the ground and commit.

In a Texas small town, like I said, gossip can run wild, and just the thought of it—real or imagined—can stop even strong people from realizing their dreams. Few things I've done in my life were more gossip-worthy than choosing single parenthood. Seriously, heading down to the local bar and having an "oops" would have been far less shocking and much more socially acceptable. As you learned in the previous chapter, the way I countered those whispers was to live loud. I put myself and my choices boldly out there, I didn't hide anything and I worked to bring the naysayers along with me. No shame, no pain, no drama; just loud and proud.

The outcome of this is that the people who have the little conversations about me, well, I never hear them. I'm too busy living loud and bringing others who want more out of life along with me. Eventually, those little conversations stop

I acted big, and got big, before I was big.

because I prove the talkers wrong. They begin to look really silly. The bubble of believers around me grows while the bubble of gossipers shrinks. That's how people who want more from life embrace new ideas and change, and I use it in my business life, too.

Getting big—thinking big *and* acting big—gives you the space to live loud and actually make your big dreams happen. It makes you actively part of the process. The dream can't possibly pass you by because, guess what? You are already living it, and loudly. At Barton Logistics, I want to create a whole company of people who live big, who live brazenly. This sets people free to design and live their lives. They become achievers. They become more accomplished and they become happier. That's increasing the good of life around me, which, as you read in the Foreword to this book, is my own personal mission.

During The Recession in 2008, most companies shrank under the pressure. They let their fear lead them. By contrast, Barton Logistics got big, even though we felt the same pressure our competitors felt during that time. We ended up growing because the rest of the world shrank. They made the choice to get small. And we made the choice to get big, and began acting big before we were.

Plenty of naysayers didn't believe in our strategy. There are probably plenty who still don't. I like to think I give those naysayers something to do. After all, the jaws need something to jack about and the tongues

Getting big is deliberately creating your own wake to walk through.

need something to wag about, don't they? In truth, I probably keep them quite busy, maybe even happy, but the group is shrinking. No one likes to be proven wrong over and over. And why was I so sure we would prove them wrong during the Recession? Because I never, ever, quit. (And neither does the Team at Barton Logistics.) That's the card I hold that the naysayers either don't know, or keep forgetting that I have.

Getting big is deliberately creating your own wake to walk through. If you are wondering whether this takes confidence, the answer is yes. But don't worry. My theory of confidence might sound familiar and not too surprising by now. First you manufacture it for the sake of the life you want, and eventually it becomes real based on your small and big accomplishments along the way.

You might be thinking, getting big sounds a little bold, even a little scary. It's putting a stake in the ground and living like you are already at the summit. Your days of idol dreaming and wishing are over, so yes, it is a question of confidence. But here again, I say confidence is a choice. Just like you can decide to achieve your dream and get big about it, you can decide you are confident, and get big about that, too.

It's putting a stake in the ground and living like you are already at the summit. Your days of idol dreaming and wishing are over ...

When I first started Barton Logistics, I didn't have as much confidence in my abilities or my company as I do now. But in those very early days, I decided the way to become confident was to act confidently. So I lived big and said things a confident person would say, I did things a confident person would do. One day I realized that it just was. That I had become the confident person I had been role-playing. That's how it works. You live big, and then you become big.

The fact is, you have to confidently own your greatness, even as it is emerging, and not be apologetic to the world because of what you will do or have already done. I don't apologize to anyone who my family or my business choices might offend. If they think my lifestyle is over the top, well, they've not seen anything yet! The point is, what they think is not my issue, other than it's my job to stay on course and live my dream. It's not wrong for them to have their beliefs, they just don't get any of my time. The people who love me get my time. The people who want great journeys for themselves get my time. Those people are, in fact, the reason I wrote this book. There are also, of course, those people who love me but whom I make very uncomfortable. I don't apologize for that, either.

Minute by minute, day by day, our constant choice is to either shrink or get big. Choose big and start behaving like you have already arrived. Like you are already there. And talk and act in anticipation of achieving your dream. Don't believe that doubting voice that says, "Who do you think you are?" Getting big, just like being loud, means hearing your own negative self-talk and silencing anything that isn't going to take you toward your dream. Getting big means being so self-aware that you can be your own coach,

Minute by minute, day by day, our constant choice is to either shrink or get big.

when your real coach isn't around. It's calling yourself on yourself, and being accountable.

I have coaches who hold me accountable, so I am well trained. I know how to hold my own feet to the fire. You can do it, too. Simply make the decision to get big; put it on the front burner and live it. When you slip—and we all slip—say, "I slipped," and move on resolute to do better in the next minute, the next hour, and the next day.

The bigger you are and the louder you are, the bigger the path or the wake that you will create for yourself to walk through. And the more likely you are to walk through it. So go ahead. Put yourself out there, put your butt on the line so everyone knows about it. Get big, and surprise! You'll make your dreams happen.

Put the words from the last chapter into action by living like you have already arrived, even if that is just assuming the posture.

Plan for others around you who know your smaller self and who try to keep you there.

Recognize that is the conflict between them staying in their own comfort zone and you stretching yours.

Keep stretching.

CHAPTER 14

TRUE UP TO YOUR WORD

When I say true up to your word, I'm talking about speaking your dream, driving the stake in the ground, and, without any further knowledge than you have right now at this second, going all in. It's called commitment. Once you do that, all that's left is the process and the journey to your commitment, and both are incredibly rewarding. The hard part is driving the stake and giving your word on something that you don't yet quite believe. Of course there will be bumps and bruises along the way, and you'll learn how to deal with them in the "F You, Resistance" chapter, but you just keep trucking forward and truing up to your word even when things go sideways. You'll discover that the rewards come also in those

Truing up is certainly about choosing your words, but it's also about how well you deliver on the actions following those words ...

difficult times, even if they are not obvious.

The only tools we have to influence anything or anyone are the words we use, and the actions we take chasing those words. But the words come first. And the way you choose your words is really important. I am very, very deliberate about the words that come out of my mouth. I know my word choices are bringing about my current reality. Many of you have heard about this phenomenon—it's called "the word becomes flesh." I read the teachings of Robert Kiyosaki, who says rich people use different words from those that poor people use. My brain could hardly let that in. I had never considered it, and this was a shocking concept to me at the time. I realized that I had been using the words of a poor person in many areas of my life. Words and phrases like, "I can't . . . ," "I'll try . . . " and "I need ..." are the words of the poor and the weak.

That had to change, and it has. Truing up is certainly about choosing your words, but it's also about how well you deliver on the actions following those words that really sets you apart from the masses. And if I'm going to true up to my words through action, I'm going to true up to words that get me where I want to go. Speaking deliberately is one of the few things we all have full control over. "I can't . . . ," "I'll try . . . ," "I need . . ." are all gone from my vocabulary. I've replaced them with "How can I . . . ," "I will . . . ," "I already have . . ." And those are just a few examples.

The hard part is driving the stake and giving your word on something that you don't yet quite believe.

Not only are the words you speak important, but so is the way you talk to yourself. They go hand in hand because what leaves your mouth is often what's in your head. I like to call those negative words "dream killers." You know them, don't you? The "I'm not good at this ..." or "I'm too busy ..." or "I don't deserve ..." It's the "I could never ..." or "Why bother ..." or "I'm too tired ..." See also "I'm too old . . ." or "Things aren't so bad . . ." or "Everything's fine . . ." These are the words that rob you of your dreams. STOP using them. Your thoughts and therefore your words are indicators of your thinking and your mental health. They produce the state of the life you are in; they form your reality. You very literally live inside of the words you have been using. If you're satisfied with that reality, no problem. However, if you're not satisfied, and you have a bigger or different dream, then you need to take a closer look at your thoughts and your words. They are your very basic and foundational building blocks. I've come to the conclusion that if my thinking doesn't serve me and my dream, then as soon as I recognize it, I shut it down. I'm not going to think the thought if I'm not empowered by it. I'm not playing into my own naysaying any more than I let others' naysaying drive my actions. It takes discipline to do this and I practice often by telling that voice, "I'm not listening to you," then choosing a more effective way to think. Remember earlier, I asked why let your limiting-moment story define you? Pick a positive moment story and let it define you. It will take you where you want to go; your limiting-moment story will only hold you back.

When you start choosing your words, planting those stakes and truing up to them, people will notice that you're headed somewhere. Believe me, they will. They will recognize your change and your progress. The world will eventually start noticing your accomplishments and will completely forget about your failures and mistakes. They will forget the challenges it took for you to get there. By then, the naysayers will have long since shut up, or they will have moved on to easier targets. You will have embarrassed them by proving them wrong. When this happens, you no longer have the time to be in those conversations, and, because you are now striving toward a new outcome, you don't have the privilege of even entertaining those types of conversations. You are too busy planting stakes and doing the fun and exciting work of truing up to them.

Truing up to your word is about as basic as it gets. It is a core tenant of a successful life. True up to your word and you'll be able to accomplish everything in this book, and your life's dreams. And incidentally, when you true up, the first person you true up to is yourself. Imagine truing up the world you live in, to the true you. You'll find that immensely powerful.

Truing up to your word is about as basic as it gets. It is a core tenant of a successful life.

Pull out that inner voice list you created in Chapter 3 and anticipate the inner dialog that will come; note that you are planting a stake and truing up to your word.

Write down those statements, and next to each one write an affirmation that kicks your inner voice's butt.

Listen to how you talk for the next forty-eight hours. How many times do you use the words *try*, *can't*, and *need*? How much of what you say is self-limiting rather than *self-empowering*?

Resign yourself to kick that language out of your life.

CHAPTER 15

A FANTASTIC EXCUSE OR A GREAT RESULT? PICK ONE.

Earlier in this book, in the chapter called "Never, Ever, Quit," I mentioned that when you make an excuse, you quit, in the moment on yourself and others. Even a good excuse, one that might be completely understandable, at the end of the day is still an excuse. Something still didn't get done. It also means you wasted a lot of time. Time you could have spent on getting the job done, whatever that job was, and making progress toward achieving your dream. Instead, however, you probably spent time worrying about that thing you needed to get done, worrying about how you were going to get it done, thinking

Even a good excuse, one that might be completely understandable, at the end of the day is still an excuse. Something still didn't get done.

about what you were going to say to those around you, angry at yourself for getting in this position in the first place, and pretty low at times in the process. Plus, you wasted time conjuring up the excuse and putting it into words, and putting energy into presenting it. Imagine all that time that you could have been spending on actually doing what you said you would do!

Living a life of excuses, even great excuses, is counter to achieving your dreams. In fact, that kind of life undermines both dreaming and achievement. It's a ripe environment for that negative self-talk we all want to avoid. You know what I'm talking about, "Dream? How can you go for your dream? You can't even get (fill in *your* blank) done! Case closed." And you resign yourself, doomed to live a mediocre life. Which, of course, is also an excuse.

"But it's a really good excuse," or the defensive, "It's not an excuse. It's just what happened." You still didn't get it done! Stop being impressed with how spectacular your excuse is and get back to your word. That's how I feel and what I say to people, including myself, when it comes to making excuses.

Here's the thing: your dream must be senior to your "stuff." You know your stuff. The family drama, the common cold, the sick kid, the car's alternator. All very important, yet subordinate to your dream, your commitment, and your result. By now you've learned to ask the right kind of questions, the kind you want answers to, rather than the kind you don't want answers to and that limit you. You remember instead of asking, "Why can't I have the life I want?" to ask, "How can I have the life I want?" Really, which question do you actually want to answer?

Are you one of those people still stuck back there on the poor, sick kid? My dream is not senior to my sick kid, Mandy. How can anything be senior to a sick kid?

Suck in some oxygen. Keep reading.

Here are a few other questions worth asking yourself: the question here is, "How can I handle my stuff without making it senior to my dream? How can I have both?" Ready for the answer? You can have both when you are committed to having both. I promise. I can also promise that your sick kid doesn't want to be a darned excuse. How about having that precious pumpkin be a *reason* to demand from that powerful brain of yours the answer to, "How can I have both?" Wouldn't the answer to that question lead to a better life for both of you? Don't have the answer yet? Keep asking. It will come to you.

Excuses seldom happen in ones or twos. Making excuses often becomes a pattern of behavior, occurring in rapid-fire, continual succession. Excuses become a part of who you are. If you find yourself in this position, you simply have to free yourself of this behavior, no excuses. In fact, start with a commitment: I have no excuse for making excuses. Just stop!

Excuses seldom happen in ones or twos. Making excuses often becomes a pattern of behavior ...

In earlier chapters I talked about driving a stake into the ground. It's important to declare your dream, drive that stake, and be loud about it. Many people need to put their dream out there for others to see so they can be held accountable. This, after all, is what sets apart people who dream from people who hallucinate. Being loud is a good strategy, so long as you spend your days proving yourself, not making excuses. When you plant your dream stake, plant your "no excuses" stake at the same time. You won't achieve the first without the second.

What we are talking about here is follow through. Consistent follow through on your every word. Even a good excuse doesn't negate the fact that you didn't get your "you know what" done. I, personally, like to be around people who help hold me accountable, and because of that I, in turn, hold them accountable. I have no tolerance for excuses, either making them or receiving them, and neither should you. They are toxic to your success.

The fact is—and the sooner you realize it, the better—excuses will get you nowhere. And honestly, anytime I've made an excuse, no matter how spectacular it was, I haven't felt very good about it. Not holding true to my word destroys a little bit of me, that I then have to build back up through strong follow through. Tearing down and building up can be a vicious cycle if it happens too often. It can keep us running fast and going nowhere. I feel like a loser not sticking to my word; don't you? If you're not quite feeling that yet, just remember, no matter how exceptional our excuses are, we lose every single time we make one. How about following through and winning?

What we are talking about here is follow through. Consistent follow through on your every word.

I know you know them: what excuses are your tried and true favs? Make a list.

Post that list so they are front and center. That way you'll hear yourself and recognize them for what they are.

Be loud about it, and have the people around you listening for your excuses and give them permission, actually demand, they call you on them.

When you eliminate an excuse from your life and your list, celebrate by crossing it off—preferably with great passion!

CHAPTER 16

LISTEN TO YOURSELF

You'll find language, either thought or spoken, a recurring theme in this book. You've heard it a few times already. The reason it is so important is, we don't often hear ourselves—we just feel the result of whatever we say, right? You might feel weak, tired, unhappy, powerless, lost, confused, or any of a host of emotions that stall your progress.

The mission of this chapter is to change that, and fully wake up your ears to self-limiting talk. If you want a shortcut to achieving success with this book, then do one thing: listen to yourself. By that I mean listen to the words you think and speak every day and be deliberate with your language. When you eliminate the words that hold you back, you're

If you want a shortcut to achieving success with this book, then do one thing: listen to yourself.

off to a great start. Allow me to be specific about three words. The sooner you completely cut out the words "fail," "try," and "need," three words I mentioned in the chapter "True Up to Your Word," the sooner you will be on track to achieve your dreams.

In the chapter, "Never, Ever, Quit," you first learned of my distaste for the word "try." Allow me to delve further in so I can make sure you dislike it as much as I do and kick it out of your vocabulary. To me, "try" instantly implies failure, and "need" keeps you there. In fact, these two words almost guarantee the third: that you will "fail." Can you see how these three words can limit your dreams and your life?

There's the old adage I mentioned earlier, "If at first you don't succeed, try, try again." We've all heard it and are taught to believe it is sage advice for persevering in life. But to me, this statement is completely counter to achieving your dreams. Before you say, "You're wrong, Mandy," think about what this is actually saying. Are you really "trying and trying again?" Or are you just doing the work on the path to achieving your dream? Your job is simply to "do" on the path to success, not "try." For too many people, the word "try" is the opposite of doing. It is, in a sense, an excuse, and an excuse is the same as quitting.

People who use conditional words like "try" and "need," in ten years will be in the same or worse shape than they are today.

Another problem with this adage? Who said you didn't succeed in the first place? You didn't quit yet. Who said the game was over and that you didn't succeed? Where do we get this crap? The only way you don't succeed is if you quit. Where did we get this crap about not succeeding? Why do we believe it, and worse yet, why do we let it lead our lives and limit our dreams?

The words you use create your tomorrow, literally. Unconditional language is the language of successful people who are going places. I want that to be you. People who use conditional words like "try" and "need," in ten years will be in the same or worse shape than they are today. They are either running in place or backing up. Certainly not going forward. I know this because I see so many people undermine their success with their words, and I coach them out of it.

Some people like to argue that "try," "need," and "fail" are necessary words that communicate reality. Well, I've got some reality for you and here's an example. Maybe you're thinking, "Mandy, I'd like to try this. I think it sounds great, but I need to take care of my family and I just can't afford to fail." Look, I'm not here to talk you out of your time-honored language, but you're making my point for me. If these words are giving you the results that you want, great. But if using "try," "need," and "fail" aren't serving you, then instead, I suggest you simply use the words "I will" and "I am."

Listen to how saying "I will" instead of "I'll try" changes everything: "Mandy, I'd like to do all of this and I *will*. I am all about taking care of my family and I'm going to make this happen. Heck, *I will* do whatever it takes; I *am* committed." That's a big difference. Can

Listen to how saying, "I will" instead of "I'll try" changes everything ...

you guess which you is going to get results? The language in the previous paragraph will absolutely keep you on the sidelines of your dream. Use the language in this paragraph, and you have made a promise to yourself that you will get up and do what it takes to succeed. Understand and take heart, because for people who actually commit and chase their words, there is no failure—unless they quit. The language in the previous paragraph gives you an out. The statement in this paragraph doesn't. This is all about boxing ourselves in to produce the lives we want.

So when you think about your dream, stop thinking and speaking in terms of trying to achieve it. Think and act in terms of "I will have it. Period." You aren't saying, "I'll have my own company *if* it all works out the first time." You aren't saying, "I'll have my own company *if* I can convince my friend to be my partner." You aren't saying, "I'll have my own company *if* I can find the money to get started." That's all conditional language—*if*—and *if* implies trying, needing, and ultimately winding up with a life full of mediocrity. Just state and stand behind your words and belief: I will have my own company. I will … I will … Drive the flippin' stake!

So when you think about your dream, stop thinking and speaking in terms of trying to achieve it. Think and act in terms of "I will have it. Period."

From the list and awareness you have from listening to yourself in Chapter 15, list the triggers for when you find yourself using the words *try*, *need*, and *can't* the most. Ask yourself why you do that. Habit? Self-pity? Lack of confidence? Making those around you feel a little bit more comfortable? What is it?

Listen for when you use the words *try* and *need* in your daily life.

Ask others around you to listen for them and explain why they are dream limiters. Teaching others will reinforce the lesson in you and help them see how important words are, particularly these.

Ask those same people to hold you accountable to eliminating them from your vocabulary, and replacing them with *I will.*

Once you start using *I will*, journal in your *Step One: Jump Notebook* how it's changing your life.

CHAPTER 17

ASKING 'HOW' IS A BUZZ KILL

People who know me have, most likely, heard me say on more than one occasion, "To hell with how!" And they know I mean it. They know I'm not just being angry or fitful because the *how* of something I want is hard to do. I really mean it, "To hell with how!" I don't care about *how* I'm going to get something done. I just know that once I commit, I am going to get it done, as God is my witness, because—as you've already learned—I never, ever, quit.

Taking that attitude toward achieving your dreams is not only powerful, it's also smart and it's freeing. I learned over the years that in deciding what you want, the *what* in the process is far more important than *how* you are going to get it done.

I learned over the years that in deciding what you want, the "what" in the process is far more important than how you are going to get it done.

I often hear, "I'm just not sure I have the confidence to ..." Or, from some of my clients of deep faith, "I guess I'm just failing at fully trusting God..." Do you hear how they're beating themselves up? Is this you? If so, let me tell you something right here and now, at the risk of us parting ways. You don't lack faith. You lack commitment! You don't lack confidence. You lack commitment!

We humans are great at this. We know deep down that when we fully commit, we're in. So we use nonsense words like confidence and faith to explain away why we don't want to commit. Don't you see, these words give us wiggle room and places to hide? Commitment does not. The trick is to catch ourselves at these tricks!

I admit, taking the step toward commitment can be nearly debilitating. It can, and often does, stop people in their tracks. That's because they think the next step is *how*, and that just freezes them up. They've already had a difficult time allowing themselves to dream about the *what*; a surefire way to seize up a dream and let it die is to worry about *how* you're going to get it done. *How* is such a buzz kill! I've seen a fear of *how* ruin people's lives, keeping them in bad situations too long, living unhappy and unfulfilling lives, feeling powerless to move in any direction—especially forward. They don't know how to get out of abusive relationships. They don't know how to get better jobs. They don't know how to make more money. *How*, *how*, *how*. So they do nothing. To hell with *how*!

I've seen a fear of *how* ruin people's lives, keeping them in bad situations too long, living unhappy and unfulfilling lives ...

What most people don't realize is that the next step isn't *how*. The next step is having the guts to fully commit to your *what*. When you have this belief, and forget about *how*, you are free to dream, decide, and commit. You suspend your fear of whether or not you can get what you want and replace it with "I will get what I want." Remember "I will ..." from earlier in this book. This is the language of winning, and, if you couple it with "To hell with *how*!" you stand a great chance of living your dream.

For example, when you know you want to get out of an abusive relationship, that's the commitment you must make. That's the dream. That's the stake in the ground. Screw the "don't know hows." The *how* will show up only after you make the commitment. It never works the other way around. You simply commit. And I mean really commit: "As God is my witness, I'm going to make this happen!" Are you that committed? Yes? Okay, NOW—and only now—may you ask, "*How* can I get out of this abusive relationship safely?" "*How* can I produce more money for my family?" "*How* can I whatever-my-big-dream-is?" And you'll get your answers. Commitment is reliable like that. Also, your brain is powerful like that.

I have a trick for getting you in the habit of believing that the *how* will naturally follow your *what*, so long as you commit. I have a conversation with myself that starts with a question: "What would I want if I had no limitations? No

What most people don't realize is that the next step isn't *how*. The next step is having the guts to fully commit to your "what."

'stuff' in the way? None of the current conditions?" Then, once I've allowed myself to choose the one thing I'd do if there were no limitations, I true up to it. That means I make it a main focus of my life and continually affirm that I will achieve this dream. I cut the crap and commit to it long before I know how I'm going to pull it off. I commit to that very thing that is mired down in the *how*. I simply jump and stop worrying about the *how*, because I know once I fully commit, *how* will become evident. Remember, resources follow commitment. And they don't follow anything except commitment.

When you have the conversation I just described with yourself for the first time, it is scary. Believe me, I know. Especially when you have to be accountable to it. When I started my company, I had fear about how I would finance it. But then I said, "To hell with *how*, I'm doing this." If I had let *how* get the best of me, I'd still be working at my corporate job. Instead, I have a successful, growing business that has enabled me to dream even bigger dreams than I'd ever imagined and create the life I really want. My unique version of it. As my standards continue to increase, life gets better and better.

So to me, fear is no excuse. *How* brings fear and *what* brings excitement. The way we get over the fear is by trusting that the *how* will become evident once we commit to our dream and true up to it. I'm over the fear of *how*. But here's a fear I'm not over: you living less than a completely fulfilled life.

What would I want if I had no limitations?

That, to me, is far scarier than the momentary fear of "Can I do this?" You can overcome self-doubt by achieving. Are you hoping an unhappy, unfulfilling life suddenly gets better or even acceptable? Well, good luck with that. I fear for you on that one.

But don't just take my word for it. Check out these words from the oft-quoted Johann Wolfgang von Goethe, the German writer and statesman. In my life, his words of truth happen over and over again: "Until one is committed, there is hesitancy, the chance to draw back. There is one elementary truth that kills countless dreams and splendid plans—that the moment one definitely commits oneself, then Providence moves, too. All sorts of things occur to help one that would never otherwise have occurred. A whole stream of events issues from the decision, raising in one's favor all manner of unforeseen incidents and meetings and material assistance, which no man could have dreamed would have come his way."

If you have to know in advance the *how* in all its buzz-kill glory, then you completely kick God out of the equation, you kick Providence out of the equation, and you kick luck out of the equation. You don't allow those things into your space. Demand *how* and you work against the universe, not with it. And then what happens? You do nothing, you forget how to dream, and you remain exactly where you are, which, if you are reading this book, isn't where you want to be.

Demand how and you work against the universe, not with it.

Give up asking *how* before you commit to "what," and you are free to dream; your dream muscle gets stronger and life gets better and better. You'll get to the point where you can see that it's just going to continue to get better. You simply know that the day you die will better than the day before. When this is your belief and reality, you give yourself the enormous freedom to pursue happiness—which is what a full life is all about.

Control freaks who can't make the jump without knowing in advance the *how* and without trusting natural laws to provide them with a path and resources, well, they are forcing themselves to stay small. They do not sit in the seat of source in their life. They have consciously chosen not to grow, to be circumstances' victim, which means they have decided against using their God-given talents to improve their lives and improve the world. Let's face it, improving the world starts with each of us improving our own life. So making the choice to stay small is a sin against God and the universe, as far as I'm concerned. It's that big of a deal.

When I started my company, I put the *how* aside and just went for it. I thought I would figure it out as I went. If I had needed to know the *how* for every decision I made, then I would have never started Barton Logistics. When people ask me, "How did you do it?" I rarely answer the question, because it's not relevant. The important point is that I followed through on *what* I said I was going to accomplish and that I trued

Give up asking how, and you are free to dream; your dream muscle gets stronger and life gets better and better.

up to it over time. When people say to me, "I don't know how you do it all, Mandy—raising two kids, writing books, running four or five businesses and a working ranch," I'm quick to turn the conversation into one about my making the decision and committing to have a happy family life; a successful workable, fun business, and life on a ranch. I'm not in the conversation about *how* hard it is to pull everything off. What conversation are you in?

I'm human. When I really stretch and dream of something, well, out of my comfort zone, I find myself worrying momentarily about *how*. The *how* will pop up periodically for all of us. So, I remind myself to take a step back from *how* because it holds me back. Two good examples are my fitness goals and finding someone to enjoy the rest of my life with. *How* am I going to get in shape after having my son? *How* am I going to find time to date? Neither of those questions is as powerful as me declaring that *I will* get in shape and *I will* enjoy dating. When I declare and commit, it happens. And so it is. I'm well on the path to fitness and I'm having a ball dating.

One other important point in this section about the buzz-kill effects of *how* pertains to leadership. If you are a leader, you will inspire no one with *how*, but you sure will inspire people with *what*. Everyone likes making something that seemed impossible possible and reveling in his or her ability to do it. A good leader puts that vision out there, inspires others to commit, then drives

If you are a leader, you will inspire no one with how, but you sure will inspire people with what.

the belief that it will happen. Leaders don't get mired in the *how* before they've built consensus around the *what*. Otherwise, we'd all just pursue what we think we can have, instead of what we actually want. Who would be inspired by *that*?

This is all about putting a stake in the ground and saying, "I will." Truing up means starting right that very moment by making the commitment to focus your life and energy on that dream. Then simply jump, and trust that the right resources and opportunities will come your way. Be patient, positive, and watch for them; then seize them without hesitation. Remember, no matter whether your dream is big or small, your ace in the hole is the fact that when you commit to your dream, you will never, ever, quit. That is fundamental to this book; make it fundamental to your life. When you do, you hold the cards. My friend Gary would say, "I sit in the seat of source, forever and ever ... amen." So do you.

Write down what you really want when you forget about the "how."

Commit to it.

CHAPTER 18

OVERCOME FEAR AND LAZINESS; REPEAT

Two of the reasons why the *how* is such a buzz-kill are revealed in this chapter. The beasts of fear and laziness are two demons that stop us from living the life of our dreams. Let's kill those beasts!

Dreaming isn't dead. Somehow we forgot or were never taught how to dream—I mean really dream. And then, on the off chance that we do have a dream, the demons fear and laziness step in to undermine us. You know what I'm talking about. We all have the fear and laziness demons in our lives to one degree or another. I certainly do.

We all have the fear and laziness demons in our lives to one degree or another. I certainly do.

I look at fear and laziness as two distinct cycles. Sometimes accomplishing my dreams gets stalled because of fear.

There's something I don't want to do or I am afraid of tackling. That's my fear cycle. At other times, my progress gets slowed because I just get lazy. That thing I want done, somehow doesn't get done. Ah ha! I'm in my laziness cycle. I've learned to recognize these two foes for what they are: just cycles that I can re-adjust and re-focus without getting so emotionally drained.

Take a look at your own life. Thinking about these two demons as cycles, can you recognize times when you have been in the fear cycle or the laziness cycle? Not sure yet?

One of the sure signs that I am treading in either the fear or laziness cycle is when my life isn't going how I want it to go. There's my red flag. Things aren't moving as fast as I feel they should. The direction is off. Or sometimes it's just pure stagnation—nothing is moving—and I'm frustrated. Have you ever been there? You may be there so often that not having life go your way is, well, your life. Maybe you've accepted that as truth and even just become used to living like that. Let me say, your life does not have to be that way. A life that makes you feel helpless, hopeless, worthless, or unfulfilled is the product of fear or laziness or both. When you conquer these two demons, by recognizing and implementing techniques to subdue them, your life will change dramatically. Understand, they will always show up from time to time. You never fully eliminate them from your life, which is okay so long as you know how to handle them.

A life that makes you feel helpless, hopeless, worthless, or unfulfilled is the product of fear or laziness or both.

When I recognize fear or laziness is running my show, I quickly change gears and get my cycle in check, meaning I get control back. Another way of saying that is, I kick my own butt. Many of you probably are in the same boat I am. If I don't kick my own butt, nothing is going to kick it for me. Actually, something might—sometimes life does it, which is an indicator I need to change, and sometimes I have to hire for it. A coach. A trainer. More on that later. You and I must own our motivation. If it isn't there, you just act in anticipation of it showing up.

You might think I'm unrealistic. Maybe I am, but I'm hung up on the belief that all of us can have a life exactly the way we want it. I'm hung up on the belief that the journey, not the end, is the reward. That excellent journey is exactly what I'm after. The better the journey, the better the reward, the better my life. Some people see that as crazy. How do I know it's perfectly tangible? I'm living it.

Every once in a while at the company or on the ranch or even while parenting my two children, I'll need to reach out to someone for help. Often, I perceive them as knowing something I need to know but don't yet. Sometimes I hesitate making the call. That's when I know the fear cycle has me in its grips, and I take quick action. You might think it's me kicking myself in the butt and making the call. I wish it were that easy.

You and I must own our motivation. If it isn't there, you just act in anticipation of its appearance.

What I do is hold myself accountable with people who serve that role in my life. For example, I am still looking for that man whom I'd like to spend the rest of my life with. I know he is not going to just knock on my door one day. In fact, if he came up the drive on a white horse, I might even shoot him. I mean, really, a white horse and a man trespassing? Scary. So I have to put myself out there and make my goal known to the universe at large. That's not appealing to me, and I have been avoiding it for years. What if having a partner slows me down? Crimps my plans? Prevents me from creating bigger and better? Wait, what if having a partner is a multiplier for me and I can do even more! These concerns and dreams aren't going away, so rather than letting more time go by without taking any action, I told my MasterMind group, "I am in the fear cycle of dating. I am getting nowhere with my dreams in this arena. I'd like you to hold me accountable to my promise of taking action." Heaven knows I don't want to walk into this group in a month with no progress to report! This group gets me out of my fear cycle by being scarier, in a way than my original fear. It's a trick I play on myself, and it works.

Sometimes I'll post my goal on Facebook, so everyone, in one way or another, holds me accountable. One goal I posted was, "I'm giving up Dr Pepper." I love Dr Pepper; I have a very long-term love affair with Dr Pepper; but if I want to get in shape and stay that way, I know drinking soda isn't helping the cause. I don't want to give it up, but I also know my "don't want tos" are a part of my fear cycle. When I hear myself saying, "I don't

I find something else that is scarier than the original fear, and for me it's not being true to my word.

want to," I know fear is involved. In this case, it was the fear of not knowing whether I could actually do it or not. After all, this was a life-long habit! Now, if I don't achieve my very public goal, well, I look pretty bad. The outcome of being a person who doesn't true up to my promises is worse than the fear of overcoming that urge for a Dr Pepper.

Before I had a MasterMind group or Facebook, I found a supportive friend who didn't let me off the hook. I passed on the ones who would wallow in my misery with me. As I quickly figured out, that didn't get me anywhere. You can always join the community at mandybarton.com if you are struggling with finding an accountability group.

It's worth noting that I often don't believe, myself, that I can achieve these big, audacious, public goals. My belief is not required; my commitment is. Same goes for you. So just take a step in the direction of where you want to go, and the path will start to appear.

Writing this book was another one of those goals that had me in the fear cycle for a long time. My limiting self-talk and excuses included, "Is what I have to say of any value? Will people find these lessons helpful? Am I being silly thinking that I could write a book?" What if they say "Who does she think she is?" So I found my point of accountability, and now here I am. Furthermore, I hate the way I sound when I hear myself saying those destructive things. They get loud in my head. Have you ever had this happen to you? Have you ever been afraid to do something different, new, or big? If so, know that everyone who wants to do something new or different experiences the same thing. There it is again, that human being thing. It means you are on the right track.

By putting myself out there saying, "I will do the scary thing," I made a promise to my MasterMind group and my Facebook followers. Being accountable to someone else helps me get over my fear, because I refuse to face these people again with nothing accomplished. This is my main trick for overcoming the fear cycle. I find something else that is scarier than the original fear, and for me it's not being true to my word. When I put myself in the situation of having to deliver on a promise, I can trick myself out of just about any fear I can imagine. What's your trick? You need to find one that works for you.

My other cycle, the cycle of laziness, can pop up any time. And just like the cycle of fear, I find myself fighting it over and over again. When it comes to laziness, I'll catch myself doing all the busywork at the office—I used to hide in my laziness by opening mail—and putting the really important stuff on the back burner. This is my laziness cycle. For a long time, opening the mail was like a comfort blanket for me, busywork that was always there for me. It's me doing the busywork and avoiding the work that I know is going to make me think, cause me a little strife, or push me out of my comfort zone. It's me getting lazy because I'm avoiding the harder work. I'm sure you've experienced this in your own work life.

My other cycle, the cycle of laziness, can pop up any time. And just like the cycle of fear, I find myself fighting it over and over again.

My personal life laziness cycle isn't what you might think. I'm not like so many people who lazily become couch potatoes. For me, the loud-and-clear signal that I'm in my laziness cycle is seeing the same personal task show up on my to-do list two or three days in a row. It might be something like cancelling a subscription, or going through my closet and weeding out things I no longer need, or getting organized for a trip, or doing my cardio workout.

To get beyond my laziness cycle, I have another trick. Whenever I find myself in this cycle, I make a rule for the next day that I can't do anything else before I get that one thing done. That's it, and I give myself no exceptions, no passes. I also put a number 2 or 3 after a task when I have to write it on the next day's list. I'm never allowed to write a 4. My rule for myself is I can't write the task a fourth time. I'll just have to go by memory if it is ever going to get done. Usually, this is enough for me to knock it out if it somehow makes it to day three. For me, it works, and the feeling I have when I get beyond my personal laziness is freeing. What will work for you?

If you are ever going to live your dream, you must discover what the fear and laziness cycles look like in your own life. They are working against you, I guarantee. So you hide in that place I call ambiguity. I am encouraging you to call yourself out. Turning on that TV? Are you watching TV or are you avoiding something you know you should do?

... the feeling I have when I get beyond my personal laziness is freeing.

If you are someone who has

allowed laziness and fear to rule your life, those habits have become flesh. Fearful and lazy may very well be who you are today. That doesn't mean that is the person you have to be tomorrow. It's up to you. The way you start to become a person who overcomes fear and laziness is to start this moment. Start now. The only thing we have is this moment, so right now draw the line, and say, "I will overcome these two demons and true up to my word." Again, and again.

Until this chapter and your new-found awareness of these two cycles—fear and laziness—which are at play in your life, you may have never viewed your life this way. The people who join Barton Logistics quickly learn that they are entering a different world. We make them very aware of how fear and laziness work on their lives, all our lives. To be successful in our company, they must figure out the games they play on themselves and devise tricks to overcome them. It takes some practice, but once they plant the stake in the ground, they become people who stick to their word. I've witnessed countless people take on their word, and change their life for the better. It boils down to integrity and honor.

You never truly slay these two demons; they're like zombies, but eventually, by recognizing them, you get quicker at realizing when you're in one of those cycles. Your objective is to find the dream you want, focus in on it, and go after it like a heat-seeking missile. When you find yourself justifying your lack of progress, that's a red flag. Fear or laziness has taken the wheel and you're not honoring your dream or your word. Cut the crap! The only reward in justifications is that you get to stay right where you are, which isn't where you want to be. So don't let yourself off the hook. Just *thinking* that you won't allow fear and laziness to rule your life again isn't enough. When you realize you're off of your word, you have to make whatever amends needs to be made to get back into action. You have to get it trued back up, and once you do, the demons start to leave you alone. One of my coaches told me that. She said they will start to leave you alone. I've found it to be true, and I'm sure you will, too, once you have your first cycle-buster success under your belt.

I want everyone to understand that we're building muscles here. It's going to take time and it's going to be a process, so be patient with yourself. I've been through dark times, extremely dark. I took a stand a long time ago that I was going to take on my own fear and my own laziness. It was at times a painful process, but I was developing a skill set. An aptitude for taking these two demons on. I just decided that's how my life was going to work for me. In time, I have largely replaced "scared" and "lazy" with "bold" and "relentless." When "scared" and "lazy" rear their heads now, they meet with a more experienced opponent and they don't get much air time. Taking on that responsibility and taking on your own fear and laziness is hard and it's not for the weak-hearted. But the rewards are huge. You just have to walk toward your goal boldly and know that you can overcome anything to reach it.

There's nothing I enjoy more than helping people live their dreams. I love helping them devise a system to catch themselves pulling one of their tricks, then turn around and change directions. Let's put up the barriers to fear and laziness and hone our demon-slaying skills.

Today, be very aware of the concepts of fear and laziness.

Think, "What tasks am I *not* doing, that I know I should be all over?"

Write down now what you just heard in your head about why you aren't doing those tasks.

Take a look at that excuse and decide whether it's fear or laziness holding you back.

Now think of your dream. What's stopping you? Fear, laziness, or both?

You are on the path to recognizing your tricks, so keep a running list in your *Step One: Jump Notebook* and the new tricks you'll use to overcome these two demons.

CHAPTER 19

TURN OFF THE IDIOT BOX—YOU MIGHT KNOW IT AS THE TV.

Just because I love helping people live their dreams doesn't mean I am easy on the people I help. You've probably gathered that by now. I know the tricks, because I've played them on myself. Especially the cycle of laziness. The truth is, often you don't set out to be lazy. Sometimes life gets you into a rut. You come home from work or a long day of school and you go straight to the Idiot Box and lose yourself in your favorite shows—for hours. And you do the same thing again the next day and the next. It really is a terrible habit to be lazy. I've been there, and it's not a healthy place.

Just because I love helping people live their dreams doesn't mean I am easy on the people I help.

I found myself firmly planted in that unhealthy place in my twenties. On my own for the first time, I had achieved my first real dream, which was to take care of myself and live fully on my own. "Did it. Okay, that's done," I thought. "Is that all there is? The rest is just life?" I didn't realize, or maybe I forgot, I could actually keep dreaming and working toward bigger goals.

In the midst of this amnesia or ignorance, whichever, I got into watching a few TV shows. They were addictive. I'd watch one episode and then couldn't wait to watch the next one, and the next, and the next. Then I got sucked into another show. Let me rephrase that: I let myself get sucked in to another show. The more TV I watched, the less motivated I was becoming. Watching TV was supposed to be relaxing, but it was engulfing, bordering on debilitating. Thankfully, I recognized the trance I was in, and snapped out of it.

My mother always referred to the TV as the "Idiot Box" when I was growing up. It turns out she was right. Seriously, y'all. Do you think the reason you never see a Viper or a Porsche advertisement on television might possibly be because their customers aren't watching it? First class vacays at 5 Stars? Private jet companies? Designer anything? It's not a coincidence that you don't find those advertisers on TV. TV is for suckers.

Do you think the reason you never see a Viper or a Porsche advertisement on television might possibly be because their customers aren't watching it?

If you made it past the last few

paragraphs without tuning me out, ask yourself these questions: How many hours a week do I spend watching TV? What is my favorite show? Why? What do I get from watching that show? What else could I be doing with that time to create the life I say I want?

Are you living your free time in front of the Idiot Box? Living TV people's lives as your own? Living for the distraction? You actually can have more than that, you know. Your dream is waiting, and the more hours you spend with "the Box," the fewer you spend investing in your life. Snap out of the habit of TV and you'll be shocked by what you can accomplish.

Turn off the TV and walk out the door. Your life is waiting for you to create it.

Unplug your TV.

Keep it unplugged.

CHAPTER 20

PUT YOUR HEAD DOWN

Once you've determined the kind of life you want for yourself, and you've committed to it, then it's time to put your head down and work your tail end off. That's why the TV is off. It's the only way dreams become realities. All the conversation about what if, should I, could I, how? That's the long road to your dream. None of those questions are relevant, and they waste a ton of time. Time that you could be not only working on your dream, but living it, too. The funny thing is, those kinds of conversations—often you have them with yourself—fall off the radar when your head is down, working, falling down, getting back up, and making progress. The focus turns away from self-doubt and onto the next thing you have to do, which, ironically, becomes clearer in the moment. Action eats anxiety for breakfast.

All the conversation about what if, should I, could I, how? That's the long road to your dream.

The point here, when your head is down, it's easier to ignore the noise and focus on achieving the goals that lead you to your dream. When I started Barton Logistics, I did it with the money I had made in stock shows. I don't mean Wall Street stock, I mean livestock. Growing up in rural Texas—Medina specifically, an hour outside of San Antonio—that's what stock is. Cows, sheep, pigs, and chickens. Although my earnings from the livestock auctions seemed like a lot of money at the time, the funds were nowhere close to the amount I needed to start a logistics company. I learned quickly with my first load, that my "float" of personal capital was in excess of my startup money. In English, that means I was strapped and couldn't float the next load until I got paid for the load I just shipped. That wasn't going to work. I had to put my head down and get busy solving the problem of fronting a lot of money and then waiting sixty to ninety days for payment.

I made it through five years of startup hell, in part because my head was down and I was working my butt off. There was no time to worry or give up. I simply didn't have that luxury. One of the reasons I started Barton Logistics was, when I was an employee at another logistics company, my brokers would be more than happy to help me with the easy loads and the easy routes. Then they'd quit on me when I called in the challenging ones. They would promise to find a driver, but in the end, they just quit. I thought, "Geez, I could probably be successful if I just

Working eliminates the negative self-talk; you're too busy for that crap.

never, ever, quit." So that's why quitting wasn't an option. It's also why I made it such an important theme in this book.

Quitting never crossed my mind. You know why? Because I was working. Working eliminates the negative self-talk; you're too busy for that crap. You are jumping, taking leaps every day. The work is building your wings on the way down, so you can soar. That's how it works. Jump, build your wings, and soar. You don't build your wings first. From there, the formula is simple: you decide to accomplish a goal toward your dream, then you get to work. That's it. Much of this book is written to help you keep on working. It's about jumping first, then cutting all the crap that keeps you from driving toward your dream. Putting your head down and getting to work is as much about working on yourself and your environment as it is working on the dream itself. So get ready to put your head down and just get to work—you're in a crisis of your own making and it's glorious. You have wings to build!

Use your Step One: Jump notepad system to start writing down your goals to accomplish your dream.

Use the system to assign a deadline as a way of keeping you on track.

Set aside a specific amount of time for putting your head down and getting work done to accomplish that goal.

CHAPTER 21

DO MORE THAN YOU HAVE TO DO

Napoleon Hill, author of the famous book *Think and Grow Rich*, affirms the concept of doing more than you have to do when he says, "Do more than you are paid to do." Hill knew a simple truth that, sadly, too many people don't know. When you do more than what is expected, you win in countless ways.

I'll never fully understand why some adults don't do more than they have to do. You'd think their parents would have instilled this in them as children. I'm a parent, too. I know how strong the urge is to protect your children. Still, parents who want to make life easy on their kids, especially as those kids enter the workforce with their first minimum-wage jobs, deny their kids the valuable lessons of

When you do more than what is expected, you win in countless ways.

how the world works. Being the parent, one can be too quick to say something like this about a demanding employer, "They're not going to take advantage of my kid." Or the parent who says to the child, "Don't let them overwork you." These are often well-intentioned remarks. But I've seen all too often the work habits and attitudes that can come from that line of thinking, especially when it is instilled early in life. When adults don't teach kids at a young age to do more than they have to do, those kids are marching head first into a life of almost certain financial struggle, not to mention struggle in all of the other arenas of living. Unless those kids pick up this vital truth somewhere along the way and put it into action, they will be drawing the short straw in life, over and over again.

So how do you change this thinking? The question is, are you doing more than you have to do in your life? This applies to everything. Besides your work, this applies to your relationships, spiritual life, finances, health, even volunteering. Yes, that too! Imagine how the world would look if everyone showed up and did only what they were supposed to do. We have so much advancement in the world, and that is thanks to people who went the extra distance over what they were "supposed" to do. Do you get the picture? This becomes a lifestyle!

Doing more than what is expected and the rewards that come with it is a natural law of the universe. I use it; I can't explain it, but I know it works.

How can I be so certain? Easy. I've witnessed the pattern in my own company and life.

I've been interviewing and employing people for a long, long time. There are those who do more than they have to do, and those who do as little as they can get away with or only what's expected of them. I can think of a lot of reasons why these people in the latter group will always struggle financially. First of all, without continual extra effort, you learn at the pace of someone who puts only the minimum required hours into a job. That puts you at a significant disadvantage over time because most certainly you'll come up against or compete for a job opportunity with people who do more than they are expected to do. They will be learning more and earning more, while becoming more proficient than you in the process. Who do you think is going to get the promotion or win the big contract? Second, the more effort you put in, the better your relationships are. People begin to see you as a rock star. Incidentally, one of those people is likely your supervisor, who has the power to promote you; or your future business partner; or your future investor. Plus, you gain a reputation as an over-achiever. That earns you respect and trust. Two vital components for success. Don't be afraid of being labeled an overachiever; I've seen too many people negatively joke about this, and they are always the ones who underperform. It's better to be the butt of the jokes. Take it as a sign that you're on the right track, and don't listen to them.

Instead of focusing on everything that's wrong, focus on everything that's right.

Over the course of the years, we've had people work at Barton Logistics intermittently who watched the clock. Without exception, their performance on the job was substandard compared to others who go above the call of duty. They don't typically last long in our culture, either, because we are too busy growing and the team just doesn't stand for it. Clock-watchers either conform to our culture of doing more than is expected, or they leave, or they get fired. We keep the type of people whom we want to be around. People who do more than they are expected to do inspire us; those who do less drag us down.

Doing more than what is expected and the rewards that come with it is a natural law of the universe. I use it; I can't explain it, but I know it works. People who are not on the clock, who get so caught up in their work that they forget about time, end up with good results. Usually, they love what they are doing, which makes the divine outcome even more powerful. When you put in the extra work, stop watching the clock, get caught up in the excitement of what you are doing, and expect a lot of good to come your way, a lot of good *does* come your way. When you skimp and do just enough to get by, when you just make your way through your day, well then, you have skimpy results in life. You reap what you sow. If you simply expect a lot of good to come your way without doing any more than you have to, the good of the universe will not find you.

... the idea of doing more than you're paid to do is bringing your A-game ... Your A-game is the price of admission to the game.

Some of the questions I often hear about this subject include, "How long does it take for all this extra work to pay off?" "When will I see the results?" "I'm not seeing any results, so is this not working?" When I hear these kinds of questions, I know I am talking with people who don't yet have the eyes to see the good of the world. They might be overly impatient, or sometimes short-sighted. Or they might not be looking for the good in the right places, so they don't see it. Remember, don't do this just to get the return. It won't work. Do it for the satisfaction of doing more than you have to.

So much of this comes down to recognizing that, no matter what's going on in your life or the world, there is always something to be grateful for. Instead of focusing on everything that's wrong, focus on everything that's right. Avoid seeing others as people who are looking to take advantage of you. As long as you are doing and learning, *you* have the advantage. After all, no one can take away what you learn. Be thankful for that. Even in my darkest times I have always had things to be thankful for. And as a family, we talk about what we are thankful for every day. I simply ask, "What are you thankful for today?" That can and often does start a whole conversation, affirming the positive. Try it now, even if you are only asking yourself. Maybe you'll be grateful that you're reading and learning from this book. I know that would sure make my day!

As long as you are doing and learning, you have the advantage. And be thankful for that.

Another important concept that relates directly to the idea of doing more than you're paid to do is bringing your A-game. I start my day and go into work every day with my A-game. For me there is no other option. Has anyone given me permission to show up with my B-game? My employees? My customers? My kids? The people I mentor? No way! My B-game is unacceptable, and so is yours. Your A-game is your price of admission to the game. That just gets you in the door, and barely. Always give 110 percent of your effort in everything you do; put in the work and reap the benefits. And do it positively. What you focus on expands. Would you rather have positivity expand, or negativity? Which one will help you achieve your dreams faster? You want the good in your life to grow, so focus on it. When you must bring up something negative, attach a positive solution. You'll be surprised at how one little shift of mindset changes everything.

When you hear your own mental or verbal voice saying things like, "I already work hard enough," or, "I don't get paid for that," or, "They don't pay me nearly enough to do that," or even those comments of martyrdom, "Good thing I was here because if it wasn't for me ...," listen to your words and ask yourself, "What am I hiding? Maybe I'm afraid to grow. Maybe I'm afraid to become something more because I'll leave friends and family behind. Maybe I'm angry at myself or others and this extra effort is just one more straw that will soon break the camel's back." Whatever it is for you, identify it so you can recognize this negative voice and do away with it. You're not doing more for them, you're doing more for you!

What you focus on expands. Would you rather have positivity expand, or negativity?

And lastly, ditch the negative people in

your life. Stop hanging around with them, listening to them, contributing to their negativism. I know you are saying, "Mandy, do you mean my spouse, children, parents, friends, aunts, uncles, cousins, pastor, etc.? Well, yes, but don't go throwing them out the door just yet. I'm not a counselor, but I would think they would support you with a loving conversation. If not, you may have to gut it up and be the one to start the change. Start sowing what you want to harvest right here and now!

Have you ever stopped to ask yourself why you are spending time with people who enjoy talking about everything that's wrong with, well, everything? Have you heard conversations at the office that sound like, "This job's okay, but ugh! Getting up to drag myself in here is murder! I mean, what choice do I have? It's another down day. Countdown to the weekend." Or worse. Challenge these people! If they're going to get space in your life, challenge them! Stand up for your positive life. Ask, "Who says you can't love what you do? Who says there have to be down days?" I always wonder who makes up this crap that the naysayers and the pessimists just keep repeating as if it is truth. And for them, it became truth. But that's not you! You made it this far into my book, so I know you are different and want to grow. Well done. Keep going. I've found that when I continually challenge their negative with a positive, they start spewing their negativity at easier targets and my positive space gets bigger.

... train yourself by doing. Wake up every day and believe that it's going to be a great day.

I have an employee who clearly loves his work and is jazzed by it, but he always ends his happy statement with a "but." "I love my work, *but* it's a lot." "I'm good at what I do, *but* I can get tired." I came to realize that he was adding the "buts" to appease the smaller thinkers in his world who were not comfortable with him loving his job. The possibility of being thrilled with one's daily work was not even on their radar. This poor guy was making excuses for being happy in his job! Can you imagine?

I can. I've done it, too. Haven't most people? Negative people make it difficult at best, and impossible at worst, for you to recognize and sometimes even experience the good in life and be grateful for it. I've actually found myself when I'm around these people forcing myself to say something negative after I say something positive because they are uncomfortable with my positivity. I don't play into that anymore; I avoid these people at every opportunity. They are energy drains and will only drag you into their own mire. Take control of your own happiness.

Finally, and this may sound overly simple, but train yourself by doing. Wake up every day and believe that it's going to be a great day. Say it out loud, and pop out of bed. Have a morning ritual that reinforces this. Your routines directly affect your happiness. This is as much about self-preservation in our rather negative world as it is about achieving your dream.

Decide whether you are doing just enough to get by or much more, and uncover your motivation for that behavior by simply asking, "Why?" If it is martyrdom so others feel more comfortable, get over yourself. If it is because you expect an instant return, you're not quite there yet. If it is because you just know it's how you succeed in life, keep going.

Get into the habit of gratitude. Ask yourself and record in your *Step One: Jump Notebook* what you are grateful for today.

Ask others what they are grateful for by making it a point of conversation at dinner, a powerful start to a meeting, teaching your children, or a way of easing a friend's woes.

Write down in your *Step One: Jump Notebook* the initials of the positive people in your life in one column and the initials of the negative people in a second column. Recognize them for who they are so you can see the impact they have in your life. Then begin to spend more time with the people on the positive list.

Pop out of bed every day and say out loud, "Today is going to be the best day of my life!" Fake it until you make it or it makes you. Even write it down so you remember it, and then do it until you don't need the note.

CHAPTER 22

MISTAKES, HURRY UP AND MAKE THEM ALREADY

Mistakes are never, ever, limiting unless you plan on quitting. And if you are set and committed to never quitting, then hurry up and get to making some mistakes. That's one thing I always knew about myself: I knew I wasn't going to quit. So if you're not going to give up, then there's nothing truly that could go wrong. You can only grow from your mistakes and improve your game. You can apply this to any part of your life.

Mistakes are never, ever, limiting unless you plan on quitting.

My second year in business, I tried to add an asset division to my brokerage—meaning having a fleet of trucks. I fell on my face. It was a disaster. I tried investing in a friend's medical billing company. I'll never see that money again. I hired a "celebrity" accountant to help me with my business. I'm lucky I was able to stay in business after that fraudulent debacle and the audit that followed.

Even after eighteen years in business, I found myself in a cash crunch not too long ago. I had made a stupid "entrepreneur vs. CEO" mistake. Each time I made these mistakes, I could have spent my time beating myself up for my stupidity. Instead, I chose to milk the mistakes for every last drop of learning they offered and kept moving.

It's funny. Even though I've been so incredibly foolish and failed so many times, by any logical standards, all people see are the successes. Successes that only came from making mistakes and learning from them. It will happen that way with you, too. Milk the learnings from your mistakes and there is no failure.

Remember, again, the opposite of success is mediocrity, not failure. Mistakes and so-called "failures" are just a part of success. So get off the sidelines, put something at risk, and get to work screwing things up. Learning your lessons, starting today, is the fastest way to succeed.

I'll cover how to avoid mistakes through mentors, but what if you've made a ton of mistakes already and you feel as though it's too late to make the most of them? Maybe you're barreling toward a watershed birthday (forty, fifty, and sixty seem to be the biggies for a lot of folks). Perhaps you feel as though you haven't accomplished what

Mistakes and so-called "failures" are just a part of success.

you could/should/would have. If you're telling yourself it's too late to improve your lot in life, go back and reread the chapter "To Hell with Naysayers" and stop being your own naysayer. If you knew the actual date and time of your death, you'd take steps to accomplish everything you could before then, right? Well, the deal is, you ARE, without a doubt, going to kick the blessed bucket sometime in the future. There isn't a single one of us getting out of this gig alive. Why not jump now? Go back to Chapter 3 if you need a not-so-gentle push off the edge.

Whatever has brought you to today isn't a terrible thing. Sometimes, the opportunities we passed up or that passed us up were the perfect necessities to hurl us onto a new, and better, course. When I first graduated from the University of Texas, I really wanted a job with the Attorney General's office. At the time, I was a part-time nanny for a family that had some pull, and they even made a few calls to help me get the position. That opportunity didn't pan out right away, so I applied for everything, and I mean everything, in the *Austin American Statesman* classified ads. I had finally, in desperation, filled out all of my paperwork to work at a temp agency when I was hired on as a manager trainee at a base of $20,000 per year. That led me to discover that freight brokers give up too easily on their customers, which led me to the first story I told you in this book about starting my business! If I had gotten that coveted job at the Attorney General's office, I'd have given it my all, but my

Whatever has brought you to today isn't a terrible thing.

amazing entrepreneurial story might have never happened. You didn't just wash up where you are. You have gifts to give the world because of your experiences that others cannot. Holding on to regret, guilt, or disappointment keeps you in the damage part of the mistake instead of the learning part. The learning part is where the gold is. My story and many others' proves that point.

You can wallow in sorrow about the roads you didn't take, or you can embrace your learnings and accomplishments and start today to build on them. Remember earlier in this book, when I told you to take note of the impact you've had on others? Or when I said to find your purpose? If you've reached a certain age, chances are you've racked up some experience and knowledge that can only come through trial and error. You've probably made a bunch of mistakes, so you can go ahead and get down to the business of living your life by design rather than by default. Own your mistakes and learn from them, and you'll find your greatness. (More on owning your greatness later in this book.)

If your atrophied dream muscle got you trapped and you feel like you've lost a decade or two or three, take heart. The best time to plant an oak tree was thirty years ago, yes, but the second-best time is today. My mother just started a business at seventy-three years old. It's time to jump. You have gifts to give this world!

You can wallow in sorrow about the roads you didn't take, or you can embrace your learnings and accomplishments and start today to build on them.

List in your *Step One: Jump Notebook* the mistakes you have made and what you have learned from them. If you've never thought of mistakes that way before, now is the time to start. You may find it hard to dredge up the past and open old wounds. Be tough and see them in this new light.

How did you wash up to the place you are today? Start crafting your story by making a list of the things that happened, and, more importantly, the things you wanted that *didn't* happen.

What learning and what opportunities would you have missed if your path had taken a different course—maybe the one you "really wanted" at the time?

What have you accomplished because you took the course you took, the one you are on right now?

CHAPTER 23

ALWAYS BE GIVING AND RECEIVING

Here's a surprise. Giving and receiving are the same thing. It's impossible to have one without the other. You might say, "I understand that. If I like to receive, it makes sense for me to always be giving. That's a choice I can make. Maybe even, heck, that's what I was taught in church. But to always be receiving? How do I make sure that happens?" Good question, easy answer. You do two things. First, as the chapter title implies, always be giving. And two, accept the gifts when you receive them.

Giving and receiving are the same thing. It's impossible to have one without the other ...

That last part about accepting gifts is important. Receiving is giving in disguise. I know that blessings are coming my way because of all that I've chosen to give, and there's more coming in the future. Giving is really the first step to building the goodness that's coming to you. Receiving takes recognizing that you are worthy of the good that is coming back to you. Many people find that hard.

I'll give you an example that is so fitting to the idea of giving and receiving, but it might leave you with disbelief. One of the biggest take-aways from my collective experiences is a simple truth that most people don't know. The way to expand your knowledge is to teach. Sounds almost impossible, doesn't it? But it's true.

You might be thinking, "How can I teach if I am just learning?" When you read the chapter in this book "Always Be a Mentor," you'll realize that there is always something you can teach, even if you are in the process of learning. I have experienced this first hand: people who give by teaching will ultimately learn faster than those who don't. I'm not an expert in investing, but I am doing it. And because I am doing it, I have experiences I can teach.

When I teach someone about money and investing, for example—which I do often thanks to what I have learned and applied from many books and seminars—the very act of teaching reinforces and expands what I know. Through talking and answering questions with others, I gain a firmer grasp, and the material gets further engrained in me. It becomes automatic and I become more effective with my own investments. Right there the act of teaching, of giving, is paying dividends. Dividends I am receiving.

Receiving takes recognizing that you are worthy of the good that is coming back to you.

In return, the people whom I teach

get an introduction to a new world. Many of them have never thought much beyond having checking and savings accounts, so the idea of creating wealth versus just depositing pay checks and paying bills is a real eye opener. One of the folks in a money class I teach at our local library said to me, "There's this whole world that I never knew existed. I can't stop thinking about it and now I'm obsessed with it!" She joined the class because she wanted to improve her life situation and now she has the tools to do it. She admitted to me that all she wanted was to do better than her parents had done in life. She's already there, so now I'm teaching her to work her dream muscle. What's next for you, Alissa?

When you give by teaching a class, mentoring, donating money, volunteering at your kids' school, or whatever, you activate the positive power of natural law in your life. What I mean is, you affect the positive side of the universal law "give and you shall receive." Many references in faith and philosophy state that what you give comes back sevenfold. I believe it because I have witnessed in my own life that you can't out-give God or the universe. So give with your heart, not for the payout; and don't hesitate to give yourself freely. You will always get out what you put out, so don't be cheap in any form. Cheap will come right back to you.

Many references in faith and philosophy state that what you give comes back sevenfold.

Through my gift of teaching, seeing people gain access to a world they didn't know was there is deeply rewarding. I get to witness that light switch go on and see families improve and do better. It's great. What happens is, first, you give your time and help to others. Then they do the same, sharing their new knowledge—knowledge they were open to receiving—and it just keeps going. Before you know it, there's a movement of people intentionally giving and receiving. You'll notice the world change around you.

It doesn't work if you don't receive. My major in college was economics. I can't say that degree has been worth much of anything in my adult life, but I do know this. Supply requires demand. Demand requires supply. Do your part—give *and* receive abundantly.

When you say this law doesn't work, you're choosing to drive that stake in the ground and you're truing up to it. You're manifesting a life in which nothing goes your way. It's a self-fulfilling statement. You're not giving, therefore you're not receiving—making real your own lack of belief. You're allowing the negative side of this law to run the show called your life. Are you happy with that? How's it working?

Regardless of what stake you drive into the ground, you end up proving this natural law one way or another. When you don't give, you don't receive; when you do give, be open to the gifts coming your way. Remember, you're the source of the "it doesn't work" mindset and behaviors. If by reading this chapter you have realized you're the non-believer, there's still good news. Just begin. Whichever you are worse at, giving or receiving, just start participating in the cycle. Give it time, and enjoy the ride.

When you don't give, you don't receive; when you do give, be open to the gifts coming your way.

Here's a final word about receiving. Receiving is equally as important as giving. It may not be better, but it is equally as important. It's the balance side of the equation. Gracious receivers provide the giver the joy of, well, giving. When you are willing to receive, it's the best thing you can do for someone who cares enough to give you something of value. How do *you* feel when your attempts to give are blown off? When you don't receive well, think about what that does to the other person. It's rejection, it's denial, it's hurtful. It's a disservice to the giver and the universe and, honestly, it's pretty despicable. Please be a gracious receiver, because when you give, there are many gifts coming your way. Don't be the one who stops the flow.

The sooner you suspend your disbelief and get on board about giving and receiving, the sooner you will see results. Then you have to be open to receiving the gifts. You'll find the results are pretty immediate, no matter what you choose.

Write a list in your *Step One: Jump Notebook* of the ways you are already giving.

Do some soul searching to find out why you are giving in those areas. Is it because you want to help? Love the work? It makes you happy? Or, is it motived to get something you want, to ease guilt, or martyrdom?

Work to banish any negative motivations by assuming a "helpfulness" mindset.

Look for new ways to give doing something you love, or something you care about, and write them down.

Be a gracious receiver. Practice by simply saying, "Thank you," when someone compliments you, gives you a gift, or sings your praises. Nothing more, no apologies, no "I don't deserve this ..." Just, "Thank you."

CHAPTER 24

ALWAYS HAVE A MENTOR

One of my favorite quotes is from Johann Wolfgang von Goethe. He said, "What you can do, or dream you can do, begin it! Boldness has genius, power and magic in it." What he's saying is, "Jump!" It doesn't have to work the first time. You don't have to be right the first time. But just Jump. The good news is, you don't have to Jump and keep going alone. You can seek out mentors along the way.

I firmly believe going it alone is one of the most foolish things a person can do. After all, I've tried the solo artist route. I know in my life I'm going to make mistakes. But I also know I don't have to make *every* mistake. I can learn from others who have been there before me. To seize the life you want, you have

I firmly believe going it alone is one of the most foolish things a person can do.

to do everything and anything you can to bring people into your life who can guide you and who will pull you up when you fall.

If it weren't for mentors in my life, I would not be where I am today. And through my drive to do anything and everything to surround myself with the right people, I have met influencers whom I never imagined I would meet. Ask yourself the question, "Who would I pull in to get me where I want to go?" And keep asking it until you get an answer. Remember, it's a universal truth that you get the answers to the questions you ask.

Some people use the terms *mentor* and *coach* interchangeably, like they mean the same thing. To me, mentors and coaches are two different types of people. I define mentors as people who have done it before, whatever *it* is, and can share their experiences. They help me avoid the pitfalls and prepare me for the hurdles. They can be tough, but my mentors don't get in my face and deal with the ugly stuff.

Coaches do that. The ugly stuff I'm talking about is all that limiting self-talk, the mind games that hold you back, and all your other stuff you fool yourself into believing is sacred. My coaches don't let me get away with anything. Sometimes they hurt my feelings, and I get mad. I seldom get mad at my mentors.

My mentors show me the path, teach me how, and save me from countless misfires.

Coaches are valuable because they help me work on me. My mentors show me the path, teach me how, and save me from countless misfires, mostly by sharing their own experiences.

After you read this chapter, stop for a moment and ask yourself if you have someone in your life whom you consider a mentor, officially or unofficially. If you do, excellent! And, hopefully, that mentor is guiding you to some goal you want to achieve. If you don't have a mentor, you need to find one. And now. You may say, "Well I haven't yet figured out what I want. I haven't decided on my dream yet, so it might be too soon for a mentor." Not at all. If I were in your shoes, I'd ask this question until I got an answer: "Who can I pull in to help me with my dream, even if that dream at this point is simply to have a dream?" Mentors help you find your path and guide you while you are on it. Sometime that first step on the path is figuring out what you want.

My mentors have helped me through sticky areas of business growth. They taught me how to lead and manage people and how to scale up a business. They've helped me with banks, attorneys, customers, and employees. You name it, I have sought out the advice of mentors who have come and conquered before me.

Even before I started my business, I met a man who owned a trucking brokerage business, and we had coffee one afternoon. I told him my plan and he shared his knowledge freely. I learned so much from him in just that one meeting. Thinking back, if we hadn't spoken I would have fallen into some significant traps that, thanks to him, were

If you don't have a mentor, you need to find one. And now.

completely avoided. I would have had to learn the hard way.

If you are resisting the help of others (and, for that matter, resisting helping others), I believe you are resisting life itself. Later, we'll talk about *being* a mentor, but for now, know that participating fully in this process creates momentum. And momentum is the holy grail of rapid progress. You are fully participating in the circle of life.

When you have a mentor (and when you become a mentor), life keeps getting better. You reach out for a mentor because that person has been through what you are currently facing. Others, who are seeking you, know that you've been in their shoes. As you discovered in the last chapter, it's a giving and receiving cycle. You are fully participating in one of the most important laws of the universe. But more on being a mentor later in this book! Let's stick with finding a mentor.

So often I'm asked, "Mandy, where do I find a mentor?" My answer is, you can find mentors anywhere. If you hear of someone local who is succeeding at something related to a dream you have, make a call. If you find a person you admire who has achieved what you'd like to achieve, make a call. If you read a book and that author provided the inspiration you needed at that moment, reach out. You might think an author is untouchable, that he or she is too busy, but most have programs and training that will get you going. Authors often even speak at those events, so you'll

If you are resisting the help of others (and, for that matter, resisting helping others), I believe you are resisting life itself.

likely get to meet them. Personally, if a book impacts me and makes a difference to me, then I boldly reach out to the author to see what he or she can offer.

I know. It's easy to feel intimidated, calling up someone you respect. But know this: often, these people are flattered. They are doing what they are doing—writing books, lecturing, building a business, whatever—because they are givers, highly motivated to make a difference. So why wouldn't they be flattered when you pick up the phone and call? Or signed up for one of their classes? Personally, I rarely turn away calls from people who say they want to sit down and pick my brain a little. Which is a huge reason I've chosen to write this book—the calls were beginning to get more and more frequent. I feel like it's my duty to share what I've learned so others can grow from my experiences. After all, I wish everyone a life of opportunity, dreams, and the realization of those dreams. That's what life is all about, and mentors can provide a nice shortcut from dream to reality. Take the shortcut.

Who in your life do you consider a mentor, formally or informally?

Set a deadline for finding and contacting a mentor; make it a goal toward your dream, and write it in your *Step One: Jump Notebook*.

Find your mentors by asking yourself:

What authors have inspired me enough to want to talk to or meet them?

Whom do I admire in the community where I live, so much so that I want to emulate them or their success?

What do I need to learn to move forward?

CHAPTER 25

ALWAYS HAVE A COACH

In the last chapter, I briefly explained the difference between a mentor and a coach. While it's important to have both, having a coach who can help you work toward your goals isn't a "nice to have," it's a "must have." I say that knowing that good coaches are not cheap, and that all you may be able to afford at the moment is me, through this book. If that's the case, then that's fine for now. It's a great start because the wisdom of many of my coaches is in this book. But the moment you can pull together enough money to fund at least six months of coaching, do it. Get a coach.

Coaches are people who get under your skin and in your head, pushing you to do what you said you would do.

I make this bold statement for so many reasons it's hard to know where to begin. And I make it having just told you to have a mentor. As you may recall from the last chapter, mentors are people who have done what you want to do and can guide you. Coaches are people you pay to stand for your commitments. Coaches get under your skin and in your head, pushing you to do what you said you would do. When you find a mentor, you are investing in your idea. When you hire a coach, you are investing in yourself and your future. In my opinion, there is no better use for your money than investing in yourself.

When I tell people, particularly women, to invest in themselves, you know that they say? It goes something like this, "Oh, I don't spend on myself. I spend on my kids. You know, school stuff, soccer, dance lessons, clothes, sneakers. I don't have anything left to spend on myself." Blah, blah, blah.

I guess deep down these people may be afraid to let a coach into their lives. Or, and I think this is the bigger issue, they don't believe enough value will come out of a coach. They don't see it as an investment; they see it as an expense. And season football tickets are much more valuable than a coach. After all, football games are fun, and you have to have some fun. I suppose coaching could be an expense if the coach's advice never gets put into action. But when it does, the returns can far outweigh the outlay of cash. And it can be fun.

When you find a mentor, you are investing in your idea. When you hire a coach, you are investing in yourself and your future.

I never felt that hiring a coach was an expense, because I knew I was going to do what I learned no matter how hard it was. And it was hard on many occasions. It still is hard because, yes, I still have coaches and they still challenge me. I would not be where I am without the coaches I've had in my life. They are far from expenses.

One coach, in particular, helped me see that the "marketplace" view of me was less than favorable. Ouch. That was hard to hear. Another told me I was playing small in a particular area and I lacked integrity because it was inauthentic. "Oh, hell, no. Did you just question my integrity?" Oh, yes. A coach will go there. Guess what? He was right. I was playing small to make people around me more comfortable. I got big quick when it was a matter of my integrity.

That's powerful and a legitimate investment. You can have the same kind of results from a coach. You really can; I'm not special. Have you ever thought that once you improve yourself, you'll be able to do a lot more for your kids? You'll be able to have things you and your family want? Have you ever thought that your world might open up, and, when it does, you'll be able to share more life lessons and experiences with your kids? If kids are your excuse, I don't buy it. You have to come up with a much better excuse than that for me to let you off the hook. Your kids are the benefactors of your coaching.

The way I see it, sustainable giving comes from surplus, not deficit. If you are barely making ends meet, you are living from deficit. If you are settling for the life you have either because you don't know how to have the life you want or don't feel you deserve it, you are living

... There is no better use for your money than investing in yourself.

from deficit. A coach can help you find the power inside yourself to live a life of surplus. And you know what you can do with surplus, right? Give it away! That's how it works! Believe it or not, you can have that life. If I can, you can.

I used to believe that I had no serious passion for anything, no real hobby, and I've come to learn just how untrue that was. I discovered a while ago that my passion, my hobby, is doing the things that will make me more tomorrow than I am today. My hobby is growing myself to new heights. It's been, and continues to be, a fantastic way to spend my time.

Perhaps, instead of immediately making yourself a priority, making yourself a hobby would be a more approachable way to move into making yourself a priority. That should get you over the feeling selfish hurdle if putting an invest-in-myself stake in the ground is too hard at the moment. Once you begin seeing how investing in yourself increases the good of life around you, you'll know that your decision and your actions were not selfish at all. You'll make it a priority because you'll find that putting yourself first created a bigger platform from which you can give to the people you love and to the world. Get in the groove of making your self-growth the No. 1 on your priority list. Everyone around you will benefit.

Get in the groove of making your self-growth the No. 1 on your priority list. Everyone around you will benefit.

Once you have decided that your own self-growth is the best thing you can do for yourself, your loved ones, and the world, you'll quickly discover doing it alone is the doing it the hard way. A coach will cut directly to where your issues lie. There are reasons you have held yourself back—even if you are successful—from more success. Is it fear? Is it the people around you? Is it guilt? A sense of unworthiness? You know your issues are there; a coach will help you pinpoint them and move beyond them. A coach will show you how to use them to your advantage. A coach may even hurt your feelings at times (mine have) until you realize he or she is right on the money. The very few times my coaches haven't been right, I've simply tried on what they said for a while and then discarded it. Next issue.

A coach won't skirt around your emotional crap, because a coach is there to make sure you get what you want out of life. That's the coach's job. If that's not happening, fire the coach. It's of no benefit to you if your coach doesn't tackle your weaknesses. A good coach doesn't make you feel wrong for being the way you are today, a good coach simply acknowledges your starting point and leads you toward your goals. You don't have time for the whole right-or-wrong conversation. You're aiming for a better life, for achievement of your dreams.

Some of my coaching came from an organization called Gap International. I took their course to help me achieve larger goals. Gap taught me, among the many lessons, that the less I believe what I think, the faster I achieve my desired

A good coach doesn't make you feel wrong for being the way you are today, a good coach simply acknowledges your starting point and leads you toward your goals.

results. Read that one more time, because you may think it is a misprint. It's not, and it continues to be a truth that is immensely worthwhile for me. Without Gap, I might actually believe the self-limiting crap I've spent a lifetime making up. That's the kind of coaching experience I want for you, and that you must have to make your dream a reality.

I'm not done. I still constantly seek out coaches for various aspects of my life, to help me in areas I want to grow. I have a coach for public speaking; that's an area I want to improve. I have a coach for naturopathy and health, so I can add life to my years as well as years to my life. I may not know what's next, but I do know that I'll need someone pushing me. It's your job to find the right coach to help you past your current struggle and toward your current dream. Then, when you achieve that dream—with the help of a coach—you will move on to the next dream. But I don't have to tell you that by now. Achievement is addictive!

Set a deadline to find a coach and make it one of the goals you write down in your Step One: Jump Notebook.

Figure out ways you can fund hiring a coach by assessing the other "necessities" you are buying and deciding what you can live without for a while.

Overcome fear and make the call.

CHAPTER 26

DON'T BE CHEAP

Cheap is a mindset and one that is guaranteed to keep you shrinking. This chapter is after the "Always Have a Coach" chapter because coaching is an expensive, but worthy, investment. You can't be cheap with your own self, or anything else. Have you ever met someone who thinks it is noble to be cheap? Maybe you're one of them. If so, you will get a serious wake-up call in this chapter. If you can't take the heat, you may want to skip it until your skin has gotten a little thicker. But do yourself a favor and read this chapter now. It will change your life.

I run across people all the time who say things like, "I'm so cheap, I would never spend that kind of money on a bottle of wine." Or, "You spent how much on that seminar? I'm too cheap to spend that kind of money on something like that."

Truth is, nobody likes a cheap person; even cheap people don't like other cheap people.

Wow! That kind of talk *reads* just as badly as it sounds when it's spoken. The truth is, nobody likes a cheap person; even cheap people don't like other cheap people. Nobody wants to go out with a cheap person. Nobody admires a cheap person, contrary to what you might think. So please, stop thinking there is virtue in being cheap. In fact, it is exactly the opposite. Here's why.

First of all, when you give cheap out, you get cheap back. It's that pesky giving and receiving cycle at work again. Yikes! It's real hard to be a giver when you're cheap. Have you ever heard someone say, "I'm frugal" like it's something to be proud of? Yuck! It is so much more important to increase your income than it is to cut your expenses. One grows your spirit and other kills it.

I know one guy who used to go to the fast food restaurant and buy one meal for himself and one for all four of his kids to split. That's being cheap. He would take disabled veterans' parking spaces, even though he never served in the military and was not disabled, rather than pay the $3 it cost to park for the day in the garage. He didn't want to pay to play miniature golf, so he would climb the fence after hours to play for free, and, worse, take his kids with him. And he's not alone. I know a woman who buys quality Blue Bell ice cream for herself and her boyfriend and the crappy store brand for her kids. That's just being cheap. Being cheap is a mindset thing, not a financial means thing. Poor people can be cheap and rich people can be cheap. In both cases they

... when you give cheap out, you get cheap back.

see the world and live their lives through the lens of scarcity and selfishness. They inhibit the flow of giving to others and concentrate instead on accumulating and hoarding. In fact, giving often stops with them. The way I see it, being cheap is like selling out on the world and all its abundance.

Let me be clear. When I say don't be cheap, I'm not talking about being irresponsible with your finances. Saving so that you can invest is important. But saving and doing no good work with it is being cheap. Even if that good work is simply enjoyment, it matters and sets up the more positive outcome of the universal truth that what you give, you get back.

When was the last time you ever heard anyone say, "So and so is so cheap, and I think that is great"? Have you ever heard anyone say that? Most likely not. People will talk about cheap people, however, and it is seldom, if ever, in a positive way. "Oh, yeah, he hardly ever leaves a tip; he's *really* cheap," a statement that is usually accompanied by an eye roll and an emphasis on "really." Is that the label you want to wear? With your friends? Of course not. There is nothing flattering about it.

So here you are reading this book about how to find and live your dream, how to create a better life for yourself and the people you care about. You're not going through all of this personal growth and change to land on the other side, more successful—and cheap. Being cheap is like selling out on yourself and selling out on

When I say don't be cheap, I'm not talking about being irresponsible with your finances.

others. And nothing will stop the flow of big things in your life faster than being cheap.

I've known people who have had to skimp for so long that once they actually gained some wealth, or even just disposable income, they can't get out of the behavior of hoarding. What they are demonstrating is a lack of belief in themselves that they are doing well and can continue to do well. Being cheap is a sign of weakness, and once in this pattern of behavior they never seem to escape it. Break that habit right now.

In some cases, people are very generous with others, and cheap with themselves. They are cheap with their bodies, their minds, and their spirit. You know people like this. They are charitable and give freely to causes and others in need, but they spend no money on their own image and appearance. This is, of course, not sustainable. They won't pay for a gym membership, a trainer, to see a doctor, or get their teeth fixed. They won't invest in their own personal growth through seminars or having a coach. They may want to, but when they learn of the cost of these services they say, "Oh, I would never spend that kind of money on myself!" That's really sad, because life is about growing and it's next to impossible to do it alone. And worst of all is being cheap with love and human connection. Cheap with eye contact, compliments, and smiles. You get what you give. Be careful, cheapskates!

You're not going through all this personal growth and change to land on the other side, more successful ... and cheap.

Again, let me point out that I am not asking you to be irresponsible with your finances, to throw money around to satisfy banal needs. Just quit being cheap with it all. I've been broke, but I have never been cheap. There is a big difference. Even when I had very little, I made sure I gave something to others and I made sure I invested in myself. I attribute a good deal of my success to that behavior and mindset. The universe has paid me and continues to pay me back for it.

Cheap parents also do great harm to their children and their children's futures. Cheap parents teach their kids to be cheap, too. They teach them unknowingly that their world is ruled by money. They raise them believing in scarcity rather than abundance. They teach them to, in essence, "Do as little as you can get away with." Would you ever *say* that to your kids? There isn't a lesson in here that will serve those children well in their adult lives. So, if you won't stop being cheap for yourself, stop this horrible behavior for your children. Cheap is a mindset. We all like value, but demanding value is very different from being cheap.

It's an abundant world or it's a scarce world in the mind of each of us. Which one you believe is blatantly evident by whether you are cheap or not. So how do you know if you are cheap? Many people think they are just frugal. Here are the classic signs of cheapness. Eliminate every one of them from your life and don't wait until you can afford it. You can't afford not to, right here and now.

I've been broke, but I have never been cheap. There is a big difference.

The Classic Signs of Cheapness

- You won't spend money on something that may make you more money.
- You never invest in courses for yourself to learn something new.
- You want others who have invested in their self-development to teach you for free.
- You buy low-quality clothing when you can spend a few more dollars and have something that lasts.
- You cringe at the cost when you spend anything on yourself.
- You do as little you can "get away with."
- You get the free app instead of spending ninety-nine cents to get it ad-free. The message? Your time is not valuable.

What message are you putting out into the world? You want abundance to flow in? Stop cheaping out and start giving. The whole dream thing doesn't work if you aren't simultaneously giving. You should always be giving. Earlier in this book, you read a whole chapter on giving and receiving. But I want to emphasize this topic here again. When I write a check for a charitable cause, I fully expect it to come back to me. I'm not keeping score; that's not why I do it. But when things come to me, I openly receive those things because I've been expecting them. I did things like help fund the high school science lab, even though it

You want abundance to flow in? Stop cheaping out and start giving. The whole dream thing doesn't work if you aren't simultaneously giving.

wasn't the best timing for me financially. In fact, that's the best time to give. It sends the strongest message about your commitment and determination. Giving is just my way of telling the universe that I'm living the life that I chose. And it's going to go the way I say it will. Giving is a huge piece of living, and so is faith because I know what I give will come back.

Bottom line is, being cheap gets in the way of the natural laws of the universe and virtually guarantees a mediocre life. You already learned why I believe the opposite of success is mediocrity. Being cheap makes it next to impossible to live up to your full potential, and it keeps you small; in fact, it keeps you shrinking. It holds you down because you give less, so you get less in return. What I'm talking about here is a mindset, and a way of being or not being. You can't afford to be cheap with your money, your time, your health, or your love. If you continue to be cheap on others or yourself, the world of success will be cheap on you. I like to think of it this way: there's never a good time for you to pull out the cheap wine.

Ask yourself the last time you ever complimented someone on being cheap or received a compliment about being cheap.

What's the last thing that you wanted that you passed up because you were being cheap?

If you realize you actually are cheap ...

Break the cycle by leaving a bigger tip next time you're out to lunch with a friend.

Buy yourself something of real quality.

Stop skimping on others.

Write a check to a charity you care about, or give a few hours of your time.

CHAPTER 27

ALWAYS BE A MENTOR

Before I move on from the topic of mentors, I wanted to say upfront, I think it's an honor and a big compliment when people ask me if they can pick my brain a little. That's why I so rarely turn away calls from people who want my advice. If I am truly living my mission of increasing the good of life around me, then guiding people is part of the job. But there is only so much time in the day, and that unavoidable limitation is what led me, in part, to write this book. I felt like I could mentor more people if all the "Mandyisms," as people call these lessons and sayings, were in one place. I want to give all of my knowledge and experiences away and keep the flow of giving and receiving going.

I think everyone has something to share, something they could give to help others.

I think everyone has something to share, something they could give to help others. The trouble is, too many people don't believe that truth. They certainly don't believe it in their own lives for their own selves. They think they are not successful enough or rich enough or smart enough or whatever enough. Fill in the blank. You may very well be in that boat, thinking, "I'm not mentor material. What could I possibly help someone with?"

There's a fallacy in that thinking. A big one. Being a mentor isn't just about sharing your successes; it's about letting people in on your times of mediocrity, too. Mediocrity, as you well know by now, is what I consider the opposite of success. Sharing your times of mediocrity, and how you dealt with them, or are perhaps currently dealing with them, is powerful. Maybe you are in the midst of living a mediocre life right now, looking for a pathway to your dream. There's a lot to share on that journey. You may be a third of the way in, aware of where you want to go, but not sure of the pathway. You can help others who are just discovering their own longing for something better and get them started. You don't have to be complete or perfect or an expert to mentor someone; we all can do it. To someone just starting, you may be just the expert they need.

I also want to stress the importance of admitting your "failures." Failures are where most of our learning and life lessons come from. When you can share your misses with others, they learn from your experiences, and that's so insightful. The only way a person could gain more insight is to go through the failure, too.

You don't have to be complete or perfect or an expert to mentor someone; we all can do it.

But when you can save someone from that pain, what a gift!

Still not convinced? Here's an easy way to start mentoring someone with this book. If after reading it, or even while you're reading it, you feel the lessons are worthy and you have connected with even one concept, pass along that learning with your friends and family. Start a book study group and work through the chapters together. That's mentoring. That's teaching. That's giving. You are sharing your awareness, wisdom, experience, and advice.

You can be a mentor on just about anything, too, which makes the whole process really fun, particularly if your mentoring relates to something you love. People will pick up on your energy if you let it show, and they will be drawn to it. Maybe you have a green thumb, you're a good cook, or maybe you're a whiz at Microsoft Excel. Offer up your help to others. You know more than you think.

The point is, you simply have to "get into the give." What I mean by that is, you have to get into the flow of giving energy. If you want to give but honestly don't think you have anything of value to pass along to someone, then volunteer for a charity, help out at the local library, or lend your time to the Big Brothers Big Sisters organization. You'll learn through that, and it may be the pathway to finding your own mentoring strengths. By bettering others, you can't help but better yourself. It's how the natural law works. And there is no greater feeling. Share your gift. You'll find that once you get into the give, you'll

You can be a mentor on just about anything, too, which makes the whole process really fun ...

start receiving right back—and don't you dare turn it away when it comes! Remember, be a good receiver! This cycle is powerful, but you have to choose to participate in it. Fully commit without expecting anything in return—that's how it works—and the rewards will come.

Write down in your *Step One: Jump Notebook* a list of a few things you think you know something about.

Write down another list of things you love doing.

And write a third list of things you've had experience doing.

See where the three lists overlap, because those are most likely areas where you can mentor others.

Now offer to help!

CHAPTER 28

TAKE CARE OF YOUR STUFF

I've noticed a lot of people don't take care of the things they have. They kind of live in a disposable world of things that aren't meant to be disposable. This behavior will undermine you achieving your dream. I love this quote:

"If you don't take care of your Pinto, you won't take care of your Rolls Royce. Treat your Pinto like a Rolls Royce." So says Marshall Sylver, the motivational speaker. "If you don't take care of your Pinto, you'll never have a Rolls Royce." So says Mandy Barton, the no-BS author who's been dishing out reality for a lot of pages now!

I've found in my life and I see it with the people around me, if you don't take care of the things you have been given, then you will stop getting.

Not that I knew Marshall Sylver's witty remark at the time, but years ago when I didn't have much money, I owned a Mercury Topaz. It was better than a Pinto, but a far cry from a Rolls Royce. I used to keep it pristine. Once a year, I would pay a lot of money I really didn't have to get it detailed so that it always felt new. Then I worked like a dog to keep it looking great. There was more to that exercise than just being able to drive a car that felt clean and new. It played on my desires for excellence and it taught me to take care of the things that I owned, which naturally attracted more to me. It also showed the natural laws at work that I can be trusted to take care of more.

I've found in my life and I see it with the people around me, if you don't take care of the things you have been given, then you will stop getting. Why? Because you can't take care of what you already have. You show it no attention or appreciation. That goes for your job, your car, your apartment, your body, your home, and anything else that you should be grateful for.

Money comes to people who treat it right, and that means taking care of the things you buy with it. It also means keeping it moving—money is called "currency" for a reason—through sharing it, investing it, spending it, and giving it away. This is more justification for my strong belief and purpose to increase the good of life around me. I can't do that if I don't take care of my stuff.

Money comes to people who treat it right, and that means taking care of the things you buy with it.

On the first day of each month, for more than twenty-three years, I have thrown away twenty-five items. That's more than 6,900 items, and counting! It could be a sock with no match, or a pan I don't use. It's an easy exercise. When I get to twenty-five, I stop until the next month. It takes five minutes. It's my "making room for abundance" practice. Keeping something I don't use or enjoy is not taking care of it. Abundance can't flow into clutter.

There's a Bible verse in Luke. It says something along the lines of, "If you're faithful with a little, you'll be a faithful with a lot. If you're dishonest with a little, you'll be dishonest with a lot." I say money amplifies what is already there, be it generosity, greed, care, or carelessness.

You're given what you can be trusted with, so if you want more out of life, learn how to handle and care for what you already have. If that means working harder, doing more than you are asked to do, so be it. And be patient, because action builds on itself. You will start noticing an internal change with every step you take forward.

Throw out twenty-five things today. Make room for abundance in your life.

Do the same thing on this day next month.

CHAPTER 29

OWN YOUR GREATNESS

All along we've been talking about things you need to do to find your dream and make it real in your life. I've made the case for finding people to help you avoid unnecessary mistakes and to help you get through your own stuff. Now I'm sharing a truth that you simply must take to heart: you'll find it next to impossible to realize your dreams if you can't find it in yourself to own your own greatness. And *that* is where that decision lies: in yourself, not in the eyes of others.

You'll find it next to impossible to realize your dreams if you can't find it in yourself to own your own greatness.

Take it from me, owning your greatness is really hard to do. But here's the thing, when you don't own your greatness, you can't own your accomplishments, you throw it all to the stars. In other words, when you achieve goals along the way to your dream, you'll feel it was luck or fate, that got you where you are. You have to own your greatness. If you choose to skip this critical step, you'll have to continually repeat the effort it took to get you to your current point of greatness. Understand? You'll have to constantly prove your current greatness to yourself and others when you don't own it. It's like being caught in a cycle. Like the Fear & Laziness cycle, it drains you if you don't recognize what's happening. Instead of your accomplishment being the new ground floor from which you rise up, it's your constant ceiling when it's unacknowledged, holding you back. You've got to own it when you achieve it. Humility is a virtue, true, but not here. To heck with being humble for the purpose of this chapter.

Not too long ago, our company was awarded a huge contract from the nation's largest retailer. Bigger than we had ever been awarded before. We were ecstatic about it, to say the least. It demonstrated an important milestone in our growth. We had to keep reminding ourselves that we earned this. The contract was not just luck, and it was not fate. The consistent hard work, the excellence that the Barton Logistics team has demonstrated over time, earned us this contract. We have to own our greatness, otherwise we won't believe we are worthy of it. And that can impact our performance and the winning of future contracts. We would have to start over instead of building upon the ground that we took.

This contract was going to stretch us. It was going to be a challenge for us to deliver within our standards. But that is precisely what we knew would take us to the next level of greatness—and when we got there, having delivered an exceptional result for our client (or learning from our face-plant, which also would propel us forward), we would have earned and we would own that greatness, too. That's how progress and growth happen. Our success has to do with our actions, with the act of creating it, not luck. Success is not a one-time event, nor is it based on luck. Make sure you're standing on your previous wins, not discounting them and starting over each time.

I see that very clearly for our company. And believe me, in our company the conversation still goes on. Part of that conversation involves getting over what other people think, or our perception of what other people think. Here's one for you, and tell me if you haven't lived or thought this while reading this book (particularly while reading the "Be Loud" and "Get Big" chapters). We discussed that if we own our greatness, put our success out there, people will think we are getting too big for our britches. And that would be a problem. We're getting too full of ourselves.

Humility is one thing, but when the tape that's playing in your head says, "I don't deserve these rewards," or, "I just got lucky," that's a problem. When it happens in my company that someone says we got lucky or we don't deserve the rewards of our greatness, I check it. I've made the decision that we are onto something

Without great outcomes and the belief you have in yourself and your abilities because of those outcomes, owning your greatness will appear egotistical.

much bigger, which is our purpose: to increase the good of life in this world. It's not just about trucks. That's the road, no pun intended, that we're on as a company and I'm on as a person. So I deliberately uncheck the box that says we got lucky. It is completely off-purpose to increasing what is good. It's the same story in your own life.

I want everyone in our company and our town, as well as you reading this book, to uncheck the "lucky" box, to *stop playing the tape!* You didn't get lucky. The work you did up to your new-found point of greatness enabled your achievement to happen. You absolutely must own that. If we don't make the decision and begin seeing the positive outcomes, the good we are doing in the world, and own the greatness that comes from it, our tapes will play all day long and they will win, leaving most of us in the mires and cycles of mediocrity that you've just learned how to break. We'll start over, and over, and over again.

But here's the trick: you can't own your greatness without great outcomes. Without great outcomes, owning your greatness is just egotistical. People will see you as self-serving and boastful. Instead, surrounded by positive outcomes *in* others and visible *by* others, people realize you are giving not getting, helping not selling, and that your intent is in the right place. You see the difference between being egotistical and owning your greatness? Do you understand why, when you are armed with

Humility is one thing, but when the tape that's playing in your head says, "I don't deserve these rewards," that's a problem.

accomplishments that have benefitted others more than yourself, you don't need to worry about what others think?

In my hometown of Medina, Texas, I don't hide the things that I have accomplished. I want to demonstrate what a better life looks like, and what it takes to get it. I want people to be free to aspire to a better life. That's truing up to my purpose. That's helping them see, perhaps for the first time, that any dream is attainable even in the middle of rural Texas. I want them to know it's available to them, too. I want *you* to know this, too, and no matter where you start, where you live, what you do, it doesn't matter. I'm here to help, and that's the purpose of this book: to light up the pathway to getting what you want and increase the good of life, not just materially, but emotionally, spiritually, and relationally. Living your dream encompasses and will deliver all those things.

My GAP group has been excellent at enforcing and driving that belief in me. They tell me that if I don't own my greatness, if I don't stop pushing play on that deriding tape inside my head, then I am out of integrity with my purpose. That truth hits home. It makes it impossible to tolerate anything less than greatness in others around me. It becomes an insult to my beliefs and a calling to help others see their own greatness.

I want everyone in our company and our town, as well as you reading this book, to uncheck the "lucky" box, to stop playing the tape. You didn't get lucky.

When you own your greatness and the longer you own it, the tapes that play in your brain go away. As I mentioned, I am still working on this. I still have some ground to take here. I take the stand that I am exceptional because that is what my next big thing requires, and at the same time recognize that the ego is making it very hard for me to accept this truth. When I do accept it fully, I will know it because the ego, that annoying tape that says, "Really, you're not that exceptional," won't play anymore. And I won't cringe at the thought of associating myself with the word "exceptional," either. I am taking a stand! And stands aren't easy, especially ones this personal that churn up all kinds of self-limiting tapes and thoughts. You know what? Me being exceptional serves the world a whole heck of a lot better than me being average. Humility is going to have to take a back seat on this one.

Furthermore, owning your greatness isn't something that you say and expect it to stick. It is something that you live and relive until it becomes a part of you. And living it is what makes it easier to say. My breakthrough was not learning, giving, and growing for myself but for creating that in others. Some time after I started my company, I made helping others to learn, give, and grow part of leading our team. For the most part, the people around me accepted it, wanted it, and will say they are better for it. But still I ask myself—again not practiced enough at owning my greatness—if I have the right to do this for others. Who am I? But then I remember. I chose to stop playing that tape! So when it plays, I say simply, "Yes, I do. I have the results to show for it. And it is my gift." That's my new tape and I am not the

100-percent owner of it yet, but I will be, certainly by the time you read this.

Here's the best part. When I am on that stand, fully owning my greatness, believing in what I do, why I do it, and who I am, and knowing I am good at it for not just my own benefit but to serve my purpose of increasing the good of life, then I get in return freedom. The freedom to be me! I don't have to hide who I am, what I do, where I live, how I live, or anything else I have.

So how do you do this for yourself? First you have to be willing to own everything in your life. Everything that is your life. Most of us are more than willing to own the stuff that's bad. For some of us this is a full-time job. But you have to be willing to own the good stuff, too. That's the hard part; we have trouble owning the good we've created in life. Corporate America teaches you to toot your own horn on a resume. But fully owning your greatness, quietly, introspectively believing it with all your soul, no one teaches you that. "I truly, authentically created this." Can you say that about the good things in your life? Tooting your own horn is the surface crap. But quietly *owning* it between you and yourself, that's how you begin.

... you have to be willing to own everything in your life ... Most of us are more than willing to own the stuff that's bad ... But you have to be willing to own the good stuff, too.

List some accomplishments that you are hesitant to own. What do you give others credit for? What do you think "anyone" could have done even though they didn't and you did? List them and practice owning them!

CHAPTER 30

SIX LEGAL PADS TO RICHES & DREAMS

Five-year planning is never as easy as it sounds. How do you know what you want your life to look like in five years? Trust me, this is going to take some work and some real dream-muscle flexing. But it will be worth it!

For years, I've been using this one process to turn my dreams into goals and those goals into achievements. I started with six legal pads stacked on my desk. These days, I use my *Step One: Jump Notebook*, which works the same way as my six legal pads.

Below is an explanation of how the not-very-fancy, tried-and-true legal-pad system works. Whether you use the *Step One: Jump Notebook* or you're not ready to jump into that, the six legal pads is a proven method.

Here we go ...

The First

On your first legal pad, describe, in detail, what you want your life to look like in five years. Be as detailed as possible. This part of the exercise takes the longest and requires some real effort on your part. Reread the Dream Muscle chapter and spend some good, quality time here.

Here's what you might ask yourself to help you find your answers:

- How old are you?
- How are you spending your days?
- How old are your kids?
- Do you want kids, and if so, by when?
- What do you weigh?
- How much money do you have flowing in every month?
- Can you do a pull-up?
- How many push-ups can you do?
- How much of the world have you experienced?

You see the idea.

The Second

On your second legal pad, create another detailed agenda for this year. Ask yourself what you have to accomplish in the next twelve months to get your five-year plan off to a good start.

> *Here's what yours might look like:*
>
> New business is bringing in $1,000 per month. Weight 150 lbs. Add on a private room to the house. Bring in $500 extra per month. Get certified to be a foster parent. Finish the manuscript. Lease out the guestroom. Etc.

Whatever it is, list it out on this legal pad. Break the five-year plan into roughly five chunks and set your goals for this year.

The Third

This legal pad is for the quarter, your next three months. The trick here is to not look at the five-year plan; we're done with that legal pad until next year. For this one, you will be referencing only your legal pad that's designated for your year goal. Break your quarter legal pad into four rough chunks and list all of the things that must be done in the next three months to make your year goals happen.

The Fourth

Legal pad number four is designated for your month. Don't look at your year to create your month, it'll be too overwhelming. Focus on looking just at your quarter, and break this legal pad into three rough chunks. Here, you will list all the things that have to happen this month.

The Fifth

This next legal pad is for your week. Make your to-do list using just your month to help coordinate what needs to be done for the week. Never look any further out than a month once you've gotten here.

The Sixth

Finally, this last one is your to-do list for today. Look only at, you guessed it, your week to help you create it. What has to happen today so you can cross off every item on your week list?

Amazingly, I've been making my five-year dreams reality for several decades now using this tried-and-true system. It's really helped me and now it will help you!

CHAPTER 31

SYSTEMATIZE AND KEEP DREAMING

Systems will set you free! Just like you learned owning your greatness will give you the freedom to be yourself, the systems you create free you up to do more and more and more. If you want to grow as a person, if you want to grow as a business, you have to systematize. It is a big step to growth. Unless you systematize everything you can, the clock becomes your barrier. You get less productivity out of those around you who can help you. You spend too much time doing the wrong things and less time doing the right things. You end up limiting your greatness and you stay where you are: small. And guess what? You never do get to that dream of yours.

If you want to grow as a person, if you want to grow as a business, you have to systematize.

But when you systematize routine activities, like paying bills, shopping, meal preparation, invoicing, etc., you spend less time on tasks that can be routinized and more time working toward your dream. Systematizing allows you to get into a groove, a cycle, that keeps going so life can keep getting better.

Long ago, I created a variance report for my personal budget and finances. That's a fancy name but a simple Excel spreadsheet. It actually started on a piece of paper with columns, that I made copies of, so if you aren't good with computers, all is not lost. I simply listed each expense by name (rent payment, electric, self-development, etc.) and the expected amount in two separate columns. The third column was for the variance when I actually paid the bill—was I positive or negative to budget? Once it was created, I just plopped in the numbers. I didn't have to go fumbling for it each month, and if a bill didn't show up for some reason or another, I could easily see that it was missing and go seeking to find it. I had a system.

In the previous chapter, you learned about my fancy six-legal-pad system to bring my five-year plans to fruition. I simply repeat my system.

As you may already know, I own a ranch in the Hill Country of Texas. There, I raise exotic African hoofstock. It's a way to keep these endangered species around, but it can be a lot of repeat work. I could do the tending to the ranch, but why would I do that when I can hire or trade with people who have the know-how and the experience to make a ranch work? And it's their dream job. It's not my dream job; for me, it is an investment and a way to preserve endangered species. But why would I want to do the parts that are someone else's passion?

When it came to the ranch or any of my business or personal tasks, it was my job to map out a process I could give others and then let them do their jobs with passion. I do the same thing when it comes to raising my kids. I love being with them, I do it as much as humanly possible, but taking care of their every single need? That's someone else's dream job. I have great people helping me—and we're one big, fully systematized family. They get to travel with us, and care for and love my kids. My point is, you don't have to do everything on your own. There are people out there you could help by giving them a job—particularly one you're not great at—that they would love. Everyone wins this way. Before I could afford to hire, I traded wherever I could. I'd bring in someone who liked to do something I wasn't all that great at, and I would return the favor to them. Are you good at ironing and your friend is good at Excel spreadsheets and budgets? How about an elderly friend who is great in the kitchen but needs someone to run her errands? She plans and packages your meals for the whole week and you pick up her groceries. You get the picture. Create systems that highlight the preferences of everyone involved.

The better your systems, the closer your dreams.

If you can't yet hire someone and you haven't figured out how to trade, no problem. You can still systematize. Your household inventory items? Those go on a repeat list. No sense in rewriting it, just check what needs to be picked up or ordered. Organize your list by section of the grocery store and shave off more time. Anything and everything you can think of to shave twenty seconds off of a task, do it. The better your systems, the closer your dreams.

If you are saying, "That's just not me," understand I'm not a naturally systematic person, I'm a free spirit. But I recognized that systematizing was necessary in order for me to focus on other bigger things. The purpose of putting systems in place is to make it so someone else can do them, and I am no longer the lid or the bottleneck. That's you, too. Stop being the bottleneck.

Some of the systems I've created, or had created, include a house manual for my home. At Barton Logistics, we have accounting procedures, and procedures for covering a freight load, etc. Now, the Barton Logistics team creates more systems as we grow. I love creating procedures so others can carry out tasks properly. I love that others around me are doing it, too. Now it's time for you to look around your world and ask, "What can I systematize?" Then create the resource that frees you up while it keeps up your standard of excellence. And that's really the key: the answers are in the manual. You are no longer the answer machine. You are, thanks to systems, free.

The purpose of putting systems in place is to make it so someone else can do them ...

List some repeat tasks in your life that you could systemize.

Get creative. What could you do? Who could you trade with? The key is to save yourself precious time to invest in your dream. Every twenty seconds you shave off is a win!

CHAPTER 32

F YOU, RESISTANCE!

I have an important final command for this book and it's, "F You, Resistance!" Anytime you set out a big dream or a big goal, you can bet money that with it will come change. And with change, you can bet even more money that resistance will rear its demon head. Okay, you've had your warning. And it's a good warning, because when you know resistance is coming, it won't catch you by surprise—which, let's face it, is a big part of its impact.

... when you know resistance is coming, it won't catch you by surprise–which, let's face it, is a big part of its impact.

I consider resistance a natural law. It's the universe's way of weeding out the weak, the ones who really aren't committed to their dreams and are therefore unworthy of attaining them. The world doesn't just hand you the keys to the palace. All those athletes and business leaders you see and hear of, who seem to have an abundance of success, didn't get there without resistance. They were not overnight successes, as so many people often believe. Anyone you see who has attained anything, has done so by persevering and overcoming resistance all along the way. You will be no different in your journey to living your dream.

I included this chapter in this book because, when you expect resistance, you are better prepared to neutralize its effects. I know this first hand. I had a resistance shocker one day many years ago when I was returning home from a weekend away at a seminar. I felt I had big goals. Big dreams! A new lease on life, motivated, and totally on fire to create a big, new life for myself. In fact, I didn't even go home, I went straight to the office, eager to put my ideas and inspiration into action right away.

When I reached the building, I found my key, put it in the lock, and opened the door. Well, I tried to open the door. What I found was my entire office flooded and the tile floor literally in rolling waves. My eyes witnessed complete devastation. My heart sank. The whole space looked like a sea of ceramic tile ripples where the flooring had popped up all over the room. It wasn't even safe to walk in the door, let alone across the room to see the extent of the damage.

I consider resistance a natural law. It's the universe's way of weeding out the weak ...

I couldn't believe it. That office was the key to me attaining a lot of my big, new goals—many of which were financial. And here was my home base, my world headquarters of my toddler-aged company, Barton Logistics, destroyed. My desk, which I was so excited to settle into that day, was across the room and inaccessible. The water floated against it along with lots of other debris. It felt symbolic.

If you are thinking insurance would cover the damage and in the meantime and I could just call someone to clean up the mess, guess again. My insurance had a significant deductible, and I had no cash. Every dollar to my name, I had put into the business. I was fully invested with no money to clean up a flood.

A normal person whose dreams were dashed by a raging river would either cry, or scream, or yell, or swear. I did the last two, but not in the way you might expect. I had never reacted like this before—to anything—so it took even me by surprise. It was visceral. I remember very clearly my first thought, "*Resistance, Darling! I was expecting you.*" Followed by—and this is important—an enthusiastic-all-the-way-to-my-tippy-toes, "*F YOU! I'm having the life I said I'd have!*" If I had been five years old at the time, I would have ended that sentence with, "So there!" I was obstinate, which I realized could absolutely work in my favor.

I set about, without drama or fanfare, to get the floor fixed FAST so I could move on. I just canned the emotion—banished any thoughts of "poor Mandy, the victim"—and figured it out. I honestly can't even recall how I pulled it off; I just got my office back together. Fast.

"Ah, Resistance, Darling! I was expecting you!"

I learned a lot from that experience. The biggest lesson was to expect resistance when I jump into the unknown world of a new risk. The next time I took a jump and resistance showed its face, I recognized it for what it was. "Ah, Resistance, Darling! I was expecting you!" And I handled it the same way: I got busy and got past it.

Some of the resistance I have faced has been easy to solve, like, in retrospect, the office clean-up. Other bouts with resistance haven't been so easy. They have jarred my very foundations of belief. A while back I had decided to make another big change, this time in myself. I set out to let myself be more vulnerable and in general more open-hearted and less guarded with the world. This was a new way of being for me that I had identified as my next hurdle to reach my next big result that I wanted. I was setting out to become someone I was not. I was setting out to become the person I needed to be to achieve the results I wanted: in this case, creating the all-in teams and deep partnerships I wanted to move my business and my life to a big new level. That required a more open me. My mantra sounded like this: "I am vulnerable. I let others in and I let what happens happen."

Well, it happened alright. My beloved fifteen-year-old niece had a tractor accident on my ranch. As a result, she lost her foot. We had never known anyone with an amputation, and it was a scary, new time for our family. As traumatic as the ordeal was, we were beyond thankful she was alive. But that was not all of the resistance.

I didn't know which way was up. Life gets really dark sometimes, doesn't it?

My sister's ex-husband, my niece's father, decided to sue me on her behalf.

It was a horrific and confusing time for all of us. It also happened to immediately follow the unexpected death of my dad, my life's hero, whom I'd been unable to save with CPR. My accounting department was an utter disaster. Oh, and I was pregnant with my son and I'd been diagnosed with gestational diabetes (meaning comfort food was not an option!). My house also flooded somewhere in there at some point, when the hot water heater busted.

Between hospitals, lawsuits, hormones, and grief, I truly didn't know which way was up. Life gets really dark sometimes, doesn't it? During the deposition phase of my niece's case, her attorney, who was representing her, was, in my opinion, very abusive to her. If not abusive, he was at the very least really mean. Just as I declared I was going to be more vulnerable, I'm faced with this awful treatment of someone I love. I'm thinking, "The world is a horrible place if this girl loses part of her leg and is now treated like this by her own attorney. Is my decision to be vulnerable a bad idea? Do I really want to do this? This can't be smart!"

I knew the universe was testing my commitment. Natural Law was making sure vulnerability and openness was something I was really committed to. It was double-checking that having all-in teams and deep partnerships was really something that I was going to demand from this world. But here's the thing. I knew some form of resistance was coming when I declared my new way of being. It didn't surprise me, and

Natural Law was making sure vulnerability and openness was something I really wanted.

I've stuck to my decision to change, let others in, and not be so guarded. I'm also happy to never relive a year like that again, though, just for the record!

Nowadays, change is a lot more fun and so is finding the resistance points. I seek resistance out like there's chocolate to be found, with energy and excitement. Where's the resistance? You can run but you can't hide. I know you're coming! I look for it. I search for it. And I slay it upon arrival. Sometimes I even take the fight to *possible* resistance points that I think *might* pop up. Now it's a game. And life is much more fun this way.

The benefits are huge. First of all, you're prepared. You don't waste time with emotional trauma. There are no "poor me" moments. It's just a clap of the hands and move on. It's that simple. Second, this is what you call a massive time saver to achieving your dream. The faster you recognize resistance is present, the quicker you can slay it and get on your way. The trick is to not let it derail you, and to emotionally prepare for it. And take it from someone who has learned the hard way, never, ever, give in to the demon of self-pity, even when it's justified.

One last note—and this is part of the fun—resistance isn't expecting you to be prepared for it. When you sneak up on resistance by expecting it, resistance can't sneak up on you. The way I see it, resistance can't screw me if I take the fight to it first!

The faster you recognize resistance is present, the quicker you can slay it and get on your way.

AFTERWORD

The biggest problem with creating the life you really want is, most people reading this book just won't do the things that I have recommended in it, starting with "Keep it on the front burner."

This is the reason most people are not successful. It's the reason their lives have a lot more wishes than results. They are given the formula to what they say they want, and then they don't follow it.

Many, many have come before me. I read their books. I took their classes. I followed their formulas. I learned. I tweaked. I made them my own. And now I'm sharing my blueprint with you.

Don't be most people. This book is dedicated to YOUR life! The one you *really* want.

–Mandy Barton

ABOUT THE AUTHOR

Mandy Barton never, ever quits. That's it. One simple premise, one strong principle that has sprouted an empire built to increase the good of life around her. That's what Mandy Barton believes in. From the moment she decided to leave her job to start her first business, at her parents' dining room table, despite having no MBA and a load of credit card debt—forward is where she headed. That was in 1997 when she founded Barton Logistics, the first of five, Mandy Barton-founded companies. She has been unstoppable since.

A true believer in people and the gifts they have to give this world, Mandy has dedicated—invested—an abundance of time into growing personally and growing those around her. Barton Logistics was the first evidence of how influential Mandy is, as her team created and adopted the company ethos whole-heartedly. Together, as a team that never, ever quits, they cultivated a culture of learning, giving, and growing. The results she saw in her team inspired her to do more.

The next thing on Mandy's path was to take the stuff that worked best for her and coach and mentor others. For Mandy, it's about teaching people how to dream, removing barriers and watching them flourish. It's what makes life worth living. She is an inspiration and a living example of what happens when you take yourself on and commit to your dreams.

As if entrepreneur, mentor, mother and author weren't enough, add community leader and rancher to the list. Mandy serves as a Director of the Medina Community Library and the Exotic Wildlife Association. During her down time, you can find Mandy and her two children on her ranch dreaming up her next move. Here, she raises wild gemsbok and kudu, two of the most enchanting species of African hoof stock. Keep your eye on Mandy Barton—you never know where she'll jump next.

MandyBarton.com
facebook.com/MandyBartonAuthor
twitter.com/MandyBarton

Made in the USA
San Bernardino, CA
20 May 2016